# Motherhood
# The Second Oldest Profession

**Also by Erma Bombeck:**

# Motherhood The Second Oldest Profession

## BY
# ERMA BOMBECK

MC GRAW-HILL BOOK COMPANY
New York   St. Louis   San Francisco
Mexico   Toronto   Hamburg   London   Sydney

2 3 4 5 6 7 8 9 D O C D O C 8 7 6 5 4 3

ISBN 0-07-006454-7

LIBRARY OF CONGRESS CATALOGING IN PUBLICATION DATA

Bombeck, Erma.
Motherhood, the second oldest profession.
1. Mothers—Anecdotes, facetiae, satire, etc.
I. Title.
HQ759.B64 1983        306.8'743        83–9813
ISBN 0–07–006454–7


Book design by Roberta Rezk

There are a lot of proper names in this book.
None of them is real with the exception of my
    mother's, whose name is Erma.
If there is a name the same as yours, it is pure coincidence.

ERMA BOMBECK

# Contents

# Introduction

I was one of the luckier women who came to motherhood with some experience.

I owned a Yorkshire Terrier for three years.

At ten months, my children could stay and heel. At a year, they could catch a Frisbee in their teeth in mid-air. At fifteen months, after weeks of rubbing their noses in it and putting them outside, they were paper trained.

Some women were not so fortunate or realistic. They viewed motherhood from a safe distance.

At a baby shower I was attending one evening, the new mother-to-be gasped, "Did you see the story in the paper about the woman who forgot one of her children in a laundromat restroom? And she dares call herself a mother! How disgusting! What kind of a mother would . . ."

"What kind of a mother would . . ." It was a familiar phrase. Ten years and three children earlier, I had used it myself with just the right blend of shock and disapproval.

Now, I personally knew seven mothers who had tried the same thing.

"Mother" has always been a generic term synonymous with love, devotion, and sacrifice. There's always been something mystical and reverent about them. They're the

1

Walter Cronkites of the human race . . . infallible, virtuous, without flaws and conceived without original sin, with no room for ambivalence.

Immediately following birth, every new mother drags from her bed and awkwardly pulls herself up on the pedestal provided for her.

Some adjust easily to the saintly image. They come to love the adulation and bask in the flocks that come to pay homage at their feet on Mother's Day.

Some can't stand the heights and jump off, never to be seen again.

But most mothers just try to figure out what they're supposed to do—and how they can do it in public.

Motherhood is the second oldest profession in the world. It never questions age, height, religious preference, health, political affiliation, citizenship, morality, ethnic background, marital status, economic level, convenience, or previous experience.

It's the biggest on-the-job training program in existence today.

Motherhood is not a one-size-fits-all, a mold that is all-encompassing and means the same thing to all people.

Some mothers give standing ovations to bowel movements. Other mothers reserve their excitement for an affair.

Some mothers have so much guilt, they cannot eat a breath mint without sharing it. Other mothers feel nothing when they tell a kid his entire pillowcase of Halloween candy got ants in it . . . and eats it herself.

Some mothers cry when their thirty-year-old daughters leave home and move to their apartments. Other mothers sell their twelve-year-old son's bed when he goes to a long scout meeting.

I've always felt uncomfortable about the articles that

eulogized me as a nurse, chauffeur, cook, housekeeper, financier, counselor, philosopher, mistress, teacher, and hostess. It seemed that I always read an article like this on the day when my kid was in a school play and I ironed only the leg of the trouser that faced the audience, knitted all morning, napped all afternoon, bought a pizza for dinner, and had a headache by 10:30.

For a long time, I was afraid to laugh at the contrast, for fear no one else would.

Anticipating the question of which mother am I in this book, I will tell you. There's a little bit of all of them in me. Rose's humor, Janet's frustration, Mary's emptiness, and oh, yes . . . Cora's awe.

All of them are real in every sense. They are not the nameless, faceless stereotypes who appear once a year on a greeting card with their virtues set to prose, but women who have been dealt a hand for life and play each card one at a time the best way they know how. No mother is all good or all bad, all laughing or all serious, all loving or all angry. Ambivalence runs through their veins.

This book was written too late for Judy, a mother in her early twenties I met a few years ago through brief correspondence. Judy was incarcerated in a Southern prison for the unspeakable crime of killing her child. Withdrawn, unable to communicate, and living in her own particular hell, she passed time in solitary confinement reading some of my earlier books. After she had read and reread them, she wrote to me, "Had I known mothers could laugh at those things, I probably wouldn't be where I am today."

What is certain is that there is probably not one of you who has not at some time of your life demanded an answer to the question "What kind of a mother would . . ." It's an old phrase, conceived in innocence, carried with pomposity, and born of condemnation. It is not until you become a mother that your judgment slowly turns to compassion and understanding.

Let none of you who read about the mothers in this book judge them until you have walked in their shoes of clay.

ERMA BOMBECK

**1**

# So You Want to Be a Mother!

One of the biggest complaints about motherhood is the lack of training.

We all come to it armed only with a phone number for a diaper service, a Polaroid camera, a hotline to the pediatrician, and an innocence with a life span of fifteen minutes.

I have always felt that too much time was given before the birth, which is spent learning things like how to breathe in and out with your husband (I had my baby when they gave you a shot in the hip and you didn't wake up until the kid was ready to start school), and not enough time given to how to mother after the baby is born.

Motherhood is an art. And it is naïve to send a mother into an arena for twenty years with a child and expect her to come out on top. Everything is in the child's favor. He's little. He's cute and he can turn tears on and off like a faucet.

There have always been schools for children. They spend anywhere from twelve to sixteen years of their lives in them, around other children who share the experience of being a child and how to combat it. They're in an academic atmosphere where they learn how to manipulate parents and get what they want from them. They bind together to form a children's network, where they pool ideas on how to get the car, how to get a bigger allowance, and how to stay home when their parents go on a vacation. Their influence is felt throughout the world. Without contributing a dime, they have more ice cream parlors, recreation centers, playgrounds, and amusement parks than any group could ever pull off.

They never pay full price for anything.

How do they do it?

They're clever and they're educated.

Some people think mothers should organize and form a union. I think education is the answer. If we only knew what to do and how to do it, we could survive.

It's only a dream now. But one of these days there will be a School for New Mothers that will elevate the profession to an academic level. What I wouldn't have given for a catalogue offering the following skills.

***CREATIVE NAGGING 101:*** Learn from expert resource people how to make eye contact through a bathroom door, how to make a senior cry, and how to make a child write you a check for bringing him into the world. More than 1,000 subjects guaranteed to make a child miserable for a lifetime. "Sit up straight or your spine will grow that way" and "Your aquarium just caught fire" are ordinary and boring. Creative Nagging gets you noticed! Child is furnished.

***SEMINAR FOR SAVERS:*** No one dares call herself "Mother" until she has learned to save and horde. Squirreling away is not a congenital talent, as formerly believed. It can be learned. Find out where to store thirty pounds of twist ties from bread and cookie packages, old grade-school cards, and boots with holes in the toe. Learn how to have a Christmas box for every occasion by snatching them from a person before they have taken the present out of it. Learn why hangers mate in dark closets and observe them as they reproduce. Mature language.

**INVESTMENTS AND RETURNS FROM YOUR CHIL-DREN:** Frank discussions on how to get your children to believe they owe you something. Each day mothers let opportunities for guilt slip through their fingers without even knowing it. The child who was ordered to "call when you get there" and doesn't can be made to suffer for years. Find out how. Special attention is paid to Mother's Day and the child who once gave a $40 cashmere sweater to a girl he had known only two weeks, while you, who have stomach muscles around your knees, received a set of bathroom soap in the shape of seahorses. Class size is limited.

**PERFECTION: HOW TO GET IT AND HOW TO CONVINCE YOUR CHILDREN YOU'VE GOT IT:** The art of never making a mistake is crucial to motherhood. To be effective and to gain the respect she needs to function, a mother must have her children believe she has never engaged in sex, never made a bad decision, never caused her own mother a moment's anxiety, and was never a child. Enrollment limited to those who have taken "The Madonna Face Mystique."

**LEGAL RIGHTS FOR MOTHERS:** Know the law. Are you required to transport laundry that has been in the utility room longer than sixty days? Do you have the right to open a bedroom door with a skewer, or would this be considered illegal entry? Can you abandon a child along a public highway for kicking Daddy's seat for 600 miles? Are you liable for desertion if you move and don't tell your grown son where you are going? A panel of legal experts will discuss how binding is the loan of $600 from a two-month-old baby to his parents when there were no witnesses.

**THE HISTORY OF SUSPICION AND ITS EFFECTS ON MENO-PAUSE:**  Due to popular demand, we are again offering this course for older mothers. How to tell when your child is telling the truth even after her nose has stopped growing. The following case histories of suspicion will be discussed: Did Marlene really drop a Bible on her foot, keeping her from getting to the post office and mailing the letter to her parents? Did twenty dollars really fall out of your purse and your son found it and kept it and didn't know how it got there? Was your son really in bed watching Masterpiece Theatre when he heard a racket and got up to discover 200 strangers having a party in the house and drinking all of Dad's beer?

Physical examination required.

**THREATS AND PROMISES:**  Four fun-filled sessions on how to use chilling threats and empty promises to intimidate your children for the rest of their lives. Graduates have nothing but praise for this course. One mother who told her daughter she would wet the bed if she played with matches said the kid was thirty-five before she would turn on a stove. Hurry. Enrollment limited.

**NOTE:**
**GUILT: THE GIFT THAT KEEPS GIVING**  has been canceled until an instructor can be found. Dr. Volland said his mother felt he had no business teaching others when he ignored his own mother.

**2**

*What kind of a mother would...*
**tip the tooth fairy?**

Donna (Donna Reed Show),
Harriet (Ozzie and Harriet),
Barbara (Leave It to Beaver),
Shirley (Partridge Family),
Marjorie (Make Room for Daddy),
Jane (Father Knows Best),
Florence (The Brady Bunch)

Among them they had twenty-two children, six husbands, and three maids. For two decades, during the Fifties and Sixties, they were role models for every mother in the country.

They looked better cleaning their houses than most of us looked at our wedding.

They never lost their temper, gained weight, spent

more money than their husbands made, or gave viewers any reason not to believe they were living out their lives in celibacy.

They never scrubbed a toilet, were never invaded by roaches, never shouted, and no one ever knew what they did between the time their families left in the morning and came home in the evening.

Every week you viewed a miracle—seven out of seven women who got their figures back after having children.

Their collective virtue was patience. There was no situation too traumatic for them to cure with milk and cookies, no problem that could not be resolved in twenty-four minutes, plus four minutes for commercials and two minutes for theme and credits.

I often wondered what would happen if one of their children had slammed a fellow student against the paper towel machine in the school restroom and extorted his milk money.

There's no doubt in my mind:

Donna would have called a family conference.

Barbara would have met Ward at the door and said, "Dinner's ready."

Shirley would have taken away his drums for a week.

Marjorie would have changed her nail polish.

Harriet would have sent Ozzie out for ice cream.

Jane would have invited the rip-offee to dinner.

And Florence would have her live-in bake extra brownies.

It was the age of God, Motherhood, Flag, and Apple Pie. All you had to do to be a mother was to put on an apron.

No one did it better than the prime-time mothers.

I was one of the not-quite-ready-for-prime-time mothers.

I never wore hose around the house all day, nor did I know anyone personally who did.

My kids were the ones the prime-time mothers forbade their kids to play with or else they would get into trouble.

I never ironed my husband's pajamas.

If I raised my hand to wipe the hair out of my children's eyes, they'd flinch and call their attorney.

We all knew prime-time mothers were too good to be true. (I once bragged that I saved a diabetic's life by throwing my body in front of a Donna Reed rerun.) But God, how we wanted them to be.

I had a fantasy once about Jane.

She had one of those pantyhose-on-backwards days. You know, the kind when you don't know if you're going or coming. Betty had borrowed and sweated in her new Christmas sweater, she discovered a nude calendar stashed between Bud's mattress and his dust ruffle, and Kathy hadn't spoken to her for three days.

Her mother volunteered the advice, "You should be more strict with those children," and the ground was real mushy around their septic tank.

The bank called and said she had written a check to cover an "overdraft," the cleaner called to say the patches fell off Jim's favorite jacket, and someone sprayed an obscene set of directions on her picket fence.

The fantasy always ended with Jane standing in the middle of the mess and delivering a four-letter word before she fell apart. I felt rewarded somehow.

Whatever the television mothers were, they got the

message across that they were doing something important. They were the hub of the family that held it all together. And it only took thirty minutes a week to do it.

It was the not-ready-for-prime-time mothers who questioned it in the late Sixties.

They questioned the long days. The lack of fringe benefits. The run-and-fetch syndrome. The question, "What kind of a day did you have?" and the answer that fell on deaf ears.

It started out as a ripple of discontent, gathering momentum through the Seventies. By the Eighties the dissidents were a force to be dealt with, as fifty-two percent of all mothers had jobs outside the home.

Whatever happened to the Insulin Seven: Donna, Barbara, Shirley, Harriet, Marjorie, Jane, and Florence? They disappeared beneath a tidal wave of reality.

Oh, occasionally one of them returns to the tube in mid-afternoon on reruns. There are few mothers home to watch them at that time, only latch-key children, eating pizza in front of the set, who must wonder what indeed they are . . . these dinosaurs in aprons who roam the Earth smiling wisely and pouring milk.

Ironically, I miss them in spite of their maddening perfection. And I envy them a little because they seemed so fulfilled.

I ask myself why. Maybe it was because they got paid so well for being a mother and the season lasted only twenty-six weeks. Maybe it was because they only had the kids for thirty minutes a week and then they could send them back to wherever they came from.

Maybe it was even a little applause when they did a difficult scene.

Or maybe . . . maybe it was because they never had to face life between the hours the family left in the morning and returned in the evening.

Prime-time mothers.

*Fade out.*

*End of show.*

*End of an era.*

**3**

*What kind of a mother would...*
**go an entire day without shaving?**

# Frank

On October 15, 1979, Frank Rutledge became the mother of Adam, fourteen; Caroline, twelve; and Teddy, age six, thus becoming the first suburban mother in Rochester with a mustache who wasn't on estrogen.

The new role came out of a conversation six months earlier, when Frank confessed he was "burnt out" from working at the ad agency. He was sick of cereal boxes that tap danced and termites wearing tutus. All he wanted to do was to stay home and work on his novel.

His wife, Ann, was ecstatic with his decision. She had missed the sexual revolution, arrived late for the women's movement, let the kids borrow her self-esteem, and refused to begin her midlife crisis until she lost ten pounds. The idea of going anyplace where she didn't have to cut up everyone's meat titillated her.

They agreed to try it for a year. Ann would go to work and sell office supplies and Frank would stay home and write. It seemed like a simple decision. After all, the President of the United States had been working from his home for years.

There were, however, a few appreciable differences.

**1.** The President of the United States was never summoned from a high-level phone conversation that could alter the course of history to hear a voice yell, "We're out of toilet paper!"

**2.** Pest-control men did not shuffle through the White House spraying his feet with insecticide.

**3.** The First Lady never called from her downtown office with instructions for him to "go to the garage. Turn the power mower on its back and just under the right rotary blade see a serial number. Copy it down and call it in to the repair shop so we won't get caught again when the grass needs cutting."

By November 22, after a month of chasing escaped gerbils and listening all day to "I'm telling," Frank ripped the blank piece of paper out of his typewriter and made a second decision.

He decided to put off writing his novel. Instead he would keep a diary on his experiences as a househusband.

It would sell. He knew it would. He couldn't go into a bookstore without seeing an entire section of books on domestic drolleries, the covers showing frazzled-looking women in aprons and dogs nipping at their heels. After all, how many men had experienced what he was going through? It would be a book of humor. He would call it, "A Frank Look at Mothering." (God, he loved the title.)

It should also be noted that on November 22, 1979, Rochester, New York, began its coldest winter on record, with eighty-nine inches of snow falling in a six-month period.

At first Frank loved the snow. Sitting at his typewriter, he would call to one of the children as they scurried past his door and patiently explain there were no two snowflakes alike. He even insisted they trace the patterns of ice that they made on the glass.

On December 3, school was closed due to "an act of God."

For the next ten days, Frank was charged with the responsibility of keeping three children from killing one another. He found himself saying nothing while watching Teddy force a button up his nostril.

He watched Caroline color his marriage license and all he could mumble was, "Stay in the lines."

He was numb as he observed the chandelier over the dining room table shake as Adam used his bed for a trampoline.

The house had wet clothes drying all over it and smelled like a wet possum in heat.

By December 30, 1979, Frank had scribbled only three entries in his diary:

**1.** There is no God.

**2.** Cute Teddy story. He can't say "spaghetti." Pronounces it "gasphetti." Needs work.

**3.** Ann got me trash compactor for Christmas. (This was crossed out and a note made, "No humor here.")

There were a few entries after that. "January 15, 1980: Loneliness in suburbs is a myth. Teddy is on half days and changes clothes eight times between 8 AM and bedtime. He has a costume for everything, from watching Captain Kangaroo to spitting on sister's dessert. I have not been alone in the bathroom since October.

"Jan. 17: Have much to learn. Beverly from next door was here having coffee when I started to clear the table and scrape leftovers into garbage can.

"She said no one throws away anything straight from

the table. It is written somewhere no one buries garbage 'before its time.' Garbage, if it's made right, takes a full week.

"Jan. 26: Tried new liver casserole from *Better Homes and Gardens* (serves six, takes sixteen minutes to make). Blew budget on mushrooms, scallions, Brie, and Cabernet Sauvignon.

"Ann had it for lunch.

"Caroline's teacher called. I'm a homeroom mother.

"Feb. 1: *Better Homes and Gardens* lied. The liver serves sixteen over a six-day period. Beverly made it too, only she left out the scallions, Brie, mushrooms, and liver.

"Feb. 27: I am losing my mind. Everyday I put a dozen or so pairs of socks into the washer. When the washer is shut off, there is only one sock left out of each pair. Adam, Caroline, and Teddy are ticked off about socks and want to know where they go. I told them they went to live with Jesus. I hate my job."

During all of March and April, Frank did not record anything in his diary. In March, the house died. It wasn't a pretty death. The dryer went out the night Teddy had a virus and threw up on three sets of sheets, the washer gave out two days later, followed by the water heater, the vacuum sweeper, and the steam iron. The car battery went dead on the very day Frank was carpooling eight seventh graders on a field trip through a meat-packing plant. And he missed "General Hospital."

Besides, no one noticed what he did. Or even cared. Ann popped in one night with three extra guests for dinner. She didn't even notice that he took the bent fork.

Spring was supposed to come to Rochester in April, but it couldn't land because of the snow. There was nothing for Frank to live for. No white sales. No sun for a tan. He was getting fat. And the kids were making him squirrelly.

One night, after Ann had missed dinner with them all week and they were getting ready for bed, she said, "Did I tell you I've been promoted and I think I'm suffering from Success Anxiety?"

"Feed an anxiety, starve a fever," mumbled Frank.

"What's wrong?" she asked.

"Nothing," said Frank. "Everything's perfect. I can't get anyone to help me void eggs for Teddy's class to decorate for Easter. I get as far as 'Could you help me suck six eggs?' and they hang up. Adam is the only fourteen-year-old in North America who does not have an alligator on his shirt and you fall asleep in a chair every night. We never talk anymore."

"What is it?" asked Ann, tired. "Do you want to redo the house?"

"That's right," said Frank. "Toss me a couple of new sofa pillows and I'll go away."

"Look, why don't you get a new hair style?"

He chewed on his fingernail. "I'm trying to let it grow. I told you that!"

"I know," said Ann. "Let's take a vacation. Just the two of us."

"May 17: Trip was a bummer. Instead of being off by ourselves, we met another couple from Ann's office. She and Phyllis talked shop all night. Jack was childless. All he talked about was sports, his job, and his boat. We had nothing in common. Besides, I missed the kids and cut it short to get back in time for Caroline's baton-twirling recital. She only touched pits once!

"May 26: God, I'm bored. Finally stored the Christmas ornaments. Beverly has decided to have the implants. I wish I could do something drastic to change my appearance. I have no appetite, I'm tired all the time, I don't feel well in the mornings, and if I didn't know better I'd think I was . . . my God, what am I saying?

"May 29: School is out for the summer. Beverly told me about a wonderful camp. It's out of the city and has fresh air and tons of activities that develop skills. It lasts for two weeks but it helps everyone to be around contemporaries and do something else besides watch game shows and eat popcorn all afternoon.

"I'd love to go, but who would keep the kids?

"Aug. 24: Can't wait for Ann to get home so I can tell her about Reflexology. A woman in the beauty shop where I have my hair cut said I can clear up my sinuses by rubbing the back of my toe. She said every organ in my body is projected onto a corresponding spot on the sole of my foot.

"Aug. 25: Ann said it's unnatural for someone to sit around playing with their feet. We don't relate to each other anymore. What I do is never important."

Late one evening in November, Frank flipped off the kitchen light and slowly made his way to the dining room table where Ann was paying bills.

"You're a fool," she said sharply. "Why don't you make the kids do the dishes?"

"Because I found a piece of gasphetti on my plate the other night."

"So, someone was a little careless."

"Ann, we use those dishes every night and we haven't had gasphetti in three weeks."

"You're going to have to learn to be firm."

"Ann," said Frank after a long pause, "write me a check."

"For what?"

"For me."

"Frank, what do you want a check for? If you need something, just take it out of household."

"I want to know that I am worth something."

"You're serious, aren't you?" said Ann, putting down her calculator.

"Do you know that one day last week I didn't hear one human voice all day? Everyone I talked to was a recording—the bank, the elevator, your office, the school, a wrong number. You used to be able to call a wrong number and get a person."

"You're tired, Frank. You should take naps."

"I cook food and someone eats it. I make beds and someone wrinkles them up again. I scrub floors and someone tracks mud on them. It never ends."

"That's what the job is all about," said Ann.

"It's not the job," said Frank. "I remember when I used to come home from work and the kids would say, 'Hi, Dad.' Do you know what they say now? They come in and look me right in the eye and say, 'Anyone home?' *I'M* HOME, DAMMIT! I'M A PERSON! And they don't see a person anymore."

Ann shook her head. "Look around you, Frank. You've got a nice home, a yard, three children, freedom to do whatever you want all day. You've got your own car, enough appliances to open up your own store, a wife who takes care of you, and a pound and a half of credit cards. I give up! I don't know what you men want!"

**4**

*What kind of a mother would...*

**go to her grave thinking ERA stood for Earned Run Average?**

# Connie

Connie paused over her job application blank and rubbed her eyes. She was tired. She should never have stayed up to watch the end of the Miss America pageant, but she was glad she did. How often do you get a chance to see history being made? Imagine. A Miss America who was only 5′2″. There really was a God.

As she resumed filling in the blanks, she saw the black that had rubbed off on both fingers. "Terrific," she said out loud. She had just smeared her eye shadow and probably looked like a raccoon. She always forgot she had the stuff on.

All of it was new to Connie. The pantyhose every day, the bag that matched something, the wrinkle eradicator that she put under her eyes in an attempt to erase the damages caused by two teenagers, and of course her new diet: one divorce and 700 calories a day.

PLACE OF LAST EMPLOYMENT. Connie could barely remember.

AGE. Somewhere between estrogen and death.

MARITAL STATUS. She spit on her finger trying to get the black to come off.

Connie had been born married. She and Martin exchanged vows right out of high school. They did everything by the book. Bought the house, had the two planned children, went to Florida on the summer rates, and saved two years for a home freezer.

She wasn't happy and she wasn't sad.

Then one day she was at the airport seeing a friend off when she overheard a woman talking about her husband who had just passed away. She said, "The house is so quiet. There is no one to talk to . . . no one to fix things . . . no one whose presence you feel as you sleep . . . no one at the table to share your food or your day and no one who makes you feel 'alive.' "

Connie froze.

The woman had just described her life with Martin!

After the divorce, she tried a variety of jobs from her home: babysitting for friends, housesitting for neighbors, and selling cosmetics on commission. (What a joke! She couldn't even eat a ham sandwich wearing lip gloss.)

She needed a full-time job. And after three months of trudging from one office to another she made a major discovery. She wasn't qualified for anything, and she had no goals.

Goals. How she wished she had one besides being able to cross her legs in hot weather. Miss Arkansas had a great goal last night. She wanted to work for World Peace and stamp out hunger throughout the world. She started to write it in, then stopped. Maybe it sounded pretentious.

Connie took a deep breath and checked her résumé. It would have put an insomniac to sleep.

"Miss Sawyer will see you now," said the receptionist.

Miss Sawyer looked like all the other personnel managers Connie had been meeting for the past several months. Her makeup was impeccable, her hair looked like an unmade bed, and she wasn't a day over twelve.

"You have no college," said Miss Sawyer.

Connie cleared her throat. "I was going to take some classes at the junior college, but I couldn't find a parking place."

"You didn't check the box marked sex," Miss Sawyer said, as if she were grading a term paper.

Connie wanted to say, "only during a full moon," but decided against it. "Female," she said. Miss Sawyer checked it off.

"Your experience is limited," she observed. "Have you no computer experience?"

"I got married right out of high school," Connie answered.

Miss Sawyer shook her head. "I'm afraid you're just not qualified for anything we have, but we'll keep your application on file and if anything comes up, we'll call you." She reached for her phone (a personnel trick), signaling that the interview was over.

Connie sat in the parking lot, her head bowed over the steering wheel. She was too angry to cry. Not qualified for anything! Who said so? A child, not unlike her own, who should have known better, said so. She had wanted to say to the infant behind the desk, "I know you! And you know me! Didn't I hold you in my arms, nurse you, powder your behind? Didn't I feed you and hang crêpe paper for your birthday parties? I went to your class plays and took your pictures and clapped the loudest. I went to your science fairs and walked for hours while you explained how bread mold can cure cancer.

"I listened to your piano recitals, balanced your meals and made out the budget. I learned how to sew and to cut hair. I helped hamburger before anyone knew it could be helped. I made a thousand decisions in one day, counseled you, kept you well, and gave you stability. I listened to you when you talked, I laughed with you when you laughed. And I cried with you when you cried. Now my whole life hangs in balance and you ask me what I'm qualified for."

Angrily, Connie got out of the car and returned to the office where she stood before Miss Unmade Bed.

"Did you forget something?" Miss Sawyer asked coldly.

"Yes. I forgot to tell you that early this morning an interviewer told me I was too quiet. Two hours later, another said my eyebrows showed negativism and wanted to know if I could drive under pressure. I have been told if I could get a number 2 license I could drive an airport shuttle or if I were a size nine, I could rent cars. An hour ago, a girl in front of me with a mouth like Emmett Kelly and an IQ the same size as her bust got the job.

"Let me tell you who I am, Miss Sawyer, and what I'm qualified for. I'm a thirty-five-year-old woman who was a professional wife and a mother for seventeen years and I was very good at it. If you will kindly get me two extra sheets of paper, I will be glad to list my background and my skills!"

**5**

# Everybody Else's Mother

She has no name. Her phone number is unlisted. But she exists in the mind of every child who has ever tried to get his own way and used her as a last resort.

Everybody Else's Mother is right out of the pages of Greek mythology—mysterious, obscure, and surrounded by hearsay.

She is the answer to every child's prayer.

Traditional Mother: "Have the car home by eleven or you're grounded for a month."

Everybody Else's Mother: "Come home when you feel like it."

Traditional Mother: "The only way I'd let you wear that bikini is under a coat."

Everybody Else's Mother: "Wear it. You're only young once."

Traditional Mother: "You're going to summer school and that's that."

Everybody Else's Mother: "I'm letting Harold build a raft and go down the Ohio River for a learning experience."

A few mothers have tried to pin down where Everybody Else's Mother lives and what background she has for her expertise on raising children. They have struck out.

The best they can come up with is a composite that they put together by pooling their information.

As close as can be figured out, Everybody Else's Mother is a cross between Belle Watling and Peter Pan. She likes live-in snakes, ice cream before dinner, and unmade beds. She never wears gloves on a cold day and voted for Eugene McCarthy. She is never home.

She's never been to a dentist, hates housework, and never puts her groceries away. She sleeps late, smokes, and grinds the ashes into the carpet with the toe of her shoe.

She eats jelly beans for breakfast, drinks milk out of a carton, and wears gym shoes to church because they're comfortable. She never washes her car and doesn't own an umbrella.

Everybody Else's Mother moves a lot and seems to be everywhere at the same time. Just when you think she's moved out of the neighborhood, she reappears. She is quick to judge and has handed down more decisions in her time than the Supreme Court has in the last 200 years. She has only one child and a friend who "was a dear" carried it for her.

She has never used the word "No."

If Everybody Else's Mother showed up at a PTA meeting and identified herself, she would be lynched.

From time to time, the existence of Everybody Else's Mother is questioned. It is probably wishful thinking. Does she exist?

Oh yes, Virginia, she really does. She lives in the hearts of children everywhere who have to believe that somewhere there is an adult on their side. Someone who remembers the frustration of needing to belong to a peer group at some time of your life to do the forbidden . . . just because it's there.

Just because one has never seen her, does that prove she's not there? Would one question the existence of monsters that appear in bad dreams or tigers that crawl on the bed in the darkness and disappear when the lights go on?

Everybody Else's Mother is very real and for a few years she's a formidable opponent to mothers everywhere. Then one day she disappears. In her place is ninety pounds (give or take) of rebellion and independence, engaging in verbal combat, saying for themselves what Everybody Else's Mother used to say for them.

It's called Puberty. There's nothing like it to make you yearn for Everybody Else's Mother. She really wasn't such a bad person after all.

**6**

# The First Day of School for "The Baby"

### WHAT DINA SAID:

"Mike, I don't know what you're scared of. Mother's going to be right here when you come home. My goodness, you've got a nice little yellow bus to ride and your own lunch box and your name pinned on your sweater. Now what could go wrong?

"You're a big boy now, and you have to act like one. You're going to make all kinds of new friends. Now you march right out there and sit on the curb and stop acting like a baby. You don't have a thing to be frightened of."

### WHAT MIKE DIDN'T SAY:

I don't know anything.

I have new underwear, a new sweater, a loose tooth, and I didn't sleep last night. I'm worried.

What if the bus jerks after I get on and I lose my balance and my pants rip and everyone laughs?

What if I have to go to the bathroom before we get to school? What if a bell rings and everyone goes inside and a man yells, "Where do you belong?" and I don't know?

What if my shoelace comes untied and someone says, "Your shoelace is untied. We'll all watch while you tie it"?

What if the trays in the cafeteria are too high for me to reach and the thermos lid on my soup is on too tight and when I try to open it, it breaks?

What if my loose tooth wants to come out when we're supposed to have our heads down and be quiet? What if the teacher tells the class to go to the bathroom and I can't go?

What if I get hot and take my sweater off and someone steals it? What if I splash water on my name tag and my name disappears and no one will know who I am? What if they send us out to play and all the swings are taken? What do I do?

What if the wind blows all the important papers that I'm supposed to take home out of my hands? What if they mispronounce my last name and everyone laughs?

Suppose my teacher doesn't make her D's like Mom taught me?

What if the teacher gives a seat to everyone and I'm left over? What if the windows in the bus steam up and I won't be able to tell when I get to my stop?

What if I spend the whole day without a friend?

I'm afraid.


## WHAT MIKE SAID:

"See ya."


## WHAT DINA DIDN'T SAY:

What am I doing, sending this baby out into the world before the umbilical cord is healed? Where's all the relief and exhilaration I'm supposed to feel? If only I hadn't been so rotten to him all summer. "Go play! Get out of the house! Take a nap! Why don't you grow up?"

I think I blew it. I talked too much and said too little. There are no second chances for me. It's all up to someone else.

Now it's my turn. My excuse for everything just got on that bus. My excuse for not dieting, not getting a full-time job, not cleaning house, not re-upholstering the furniture, not going back to school, not having order in my life, not cleaning the oven.

It's the end of an era. Now what do I do for the next twenty years of my life?

These walls have been so safe for the last few years. I didn't have to prove anything to anyone. Now I feel vulnerable.

What if I apply for a job and no one wants me?

What if changing toilet paper spindles is my maximum skill?

What if I'm kidding myself about writing the book that I told everyone is inside me?

What if I can't let go of my past? It's only 8:15 in the morning.

I'm afraid.

**7**

# Pacifier Pioneers

A group of mothers was discussing the ten most significant contributions to the quality of their lives one night. Most of the suggestions were quite predictable: penicillin, fire, electricity, the automobile, not to mention The Pill, polyester, and ten-foot phone cords.

I don't care what women say, the number one choice for me is the pacifier. How many women would be with us today were it not for that little rubber-plastic nipple that you jammed in a baby's face to keep him from crying?

Today, it's as much a part of a baby's face as his nose or ears, but thirty years ago the pacifier was considered a maternal crutch, a visual that screamed to the world "I can't cope."

I was a closet pacifier advocate. So were most of my friends. Unknown to our mothers, we owned thirty or forty of those little suckers that were placed strategically around the house so a cry could be silenced in less than thirty seconds. Even though bottles were boiled, rooms disinfected, and germs fought one on one, no one seemed to care where the pacifier had been.

We found them under beds, buried in sofa cushions,

thrown in ashtrays and lost in the garbage. No child ever got sick from "fooler around the mouth."

I kept the pacifier a secret from my mother for as long as I could. But one day she dropped by unexpectedly and demanded, "What is this?"

"It's a pacifier."

"Do you know that if you keep using this pacifier, by the time this baby is four years old, her teeth will come in crooked and her mouth will have a permanent pout?"

"Do you know, Mother, if I do not use that pacifier, I may never permit her to become four?"

We American pioneers of the pacifier have given it the respectability it deserves. After all, what other force in the world has the power to heal, stop tears, end suffering, sustain life, restore world peace, and is the elixir that grants mothers everywhere the opportunity to sleep . . . perchance to dream?

**8**

# Who Are Harder to Raise... Boys or Girls?

If you want to stir up a hornet's nest, just ask mothers, "Who are harder to raise—boys or girls?"

The answer will depend on whether they're raising boys or girls.

I've had both, so I'll settle the argument once and for all. It's girls.

With boys you always know where you stand. Right in the path of a hurricane. It's all there. The fruit flies hovering over their waste can, the hamster trying to escape to cleaner air, the bedrooms decorated in Early Bus Station Restroom.

With girls, everything looks great on the surface. But beware of drawers that won't open. They contain a three-month supply of dirty underwear, unwashed hose, and rubber bands with blobs of hair in them.

You have to wonder about a girl's bedroom when you go in to make her bed and her dolls have a look of fear and disbelief in their eyes.

A mother once wrote me to agree. She said that "after giving birth to three boys, I finally got a girl on my fourth try. At first, she did all the sweet little things I longed to see. She played coy, put her hands to her face when she laughed and batted her eyes like Miss Congeniality.

"Then she turned fourteen months and she struck like a hurricane. When she discovered she could no longer sail down the bannister and make my hair stand on end, she turned to streaking. I'd dress her ever so sweetly and go to the breakfast dishes. Before one glass was washed, she'd strip, unlock the door and start cruising the neighborhood. One day, the dry cleaner made a delivery and said, 'My goodness, I hardly recognized Stacy with her clothes on.'

"As she got older, she opened her brother's head with a bottle opener for taking her dolls and called the school principal a 'thug' to his face.

"I am pregnant again. I sleep with a football under my pillow each night."

I knew of another mother who said, "Boys are honest. Whenever you yell upstairs, 'What's all that thumping about?' you get an up front reply, 'Joey threw the cat down the clothes chute. It was cool.'

"When my daughter is upstairs playing with her dolls I yell, 'What are you girls doing?' She answers sweetly, 'Nothing.'

"I have to find out for myself that they're making cookies out of my new bath powder and a $12.50 jar of moisturizer.

"Her pediatrician advised me to 'not notice' when she insisted on wearing her favorite outfit for four months. How do you ignore a long dress with a ripped ruffle, holes in the elbow and a Burger King crown? How would you handle it if you were in a supermarket and the loudspeaker announced, '*Attention Shoppers*. We have a small child in produce wearing a long pink dress with a gauze apron, glittery shoes and a Burger King crown'? Our third child was born recently. Another girl. I told the orderly to pass maternity and go straight to geriatrics. I rest my case. God knows it's the only rest I've had in six years."

Whether mothers want to believe it or not, they compete with their daughters. They recognize in them every feminine wile in the book because they've used it themselves. It worked on "Daddy" when you used it, and it'll work again with your daughter. ("Daddy, you do believe that a tree can swerve right out in front of a car, don't you?")

Girls mature faster than boys, cost more to raise, and statistics show that the old saw about girls not knowing about money and figures is a myth. Girls start to outspend boys before puberty—and they manage to maintain this lead until death or an ugly credit manager, whichever comes first. Males are born with a closed fist. Girls are born with the left hand cramped in a position the size of an American Express card.

Whenever a girl sees a sign reading, "Sale, Going Out of Business, Liquidation," saliva begins to form in her mouth, the palms of her hands perspire and the pituitary gland says, "Go, Mama."

In the male, it is quite a different story. He has a gland that follows a muscle from the right arm down to the base of his billfold pocket. It's called "cheap."

Girls can slam a door louder, beg longer, turn tears on and off like a faucet, and invented the term, "You don't trust me."

So much for "sugar and spice and everything nice" and "snips and snails and puppydog tails."

**9**

*What kind of a mother . . .*
### runs a wedding—in three hours,
### forty-three minutes
### and sixteen seconds?

# Donna

It was the moment every mother of the Seventies prayed for.

The phone rang and the voice said, "Mom, guess what? Barry and I are getting married!" (Hallelujah!)

Married. Her friend, Sophie, had a son who had short hair, but he wasn't . . . married. Another friend, Eileen, could boast a daughter who still shaved her legs and waited for someone to open the car door for her, but even she wasn't . . . married.

Married. It was like a dream come true for Donna. Just think, soon her little girl would have unpaid bills, unplanned babies, calls from the bank, and substandard housing. All the things a mother dreams of for her child.

Not only that, Donna would become the first mother-in-law in her bridge club. She couldn't believe that after two years of cohabitation, it was finally happening.

Then Donna hesitated. What if this were another "commitment"? Her mind raced to a meadow. A van painted with serpents. Grace Slick coming from a tape deck. Organic juice out of Dixie cups. Guests smoking the lawn.

As if she were reading her mother's mind, Lynn said, "Don't worry, Mom. It's going to be a traditional wedding."

Tears welled in Donna's eyes. A real wedding. Stuffed mushrooms, cutaways. A string quartet. Silver pattern. Tapered candles. Barry Manilow. Navel-length corsages.

The bride-to-be's father was less exuberant. "Who's Barry?" he asked.

"I forgot to ask."

"What do we know about him?"

"What's to know? He's the man who's going to marry (hallelujah!) our daughter."

"He has some nerve, after they've been living together all these years."

The invitation arrived within the week. It was shaped like a runner's shoe.

*Lynn and Barry*
*Invite You to Their*
*Marathon of Nuptials*
*Saturday, June 18, at 2 PM*
*at Jackie's Body Shop.*
*Guests will assemble in Central*
*Park and run 10 K's with the*
*bride and groom to Jackie's place.*
*Dress optional: Running or aerobics attire.*

Donna and Mel looked at the invitation in silence. They were stunned. Mel spoke first. "This isn't an invitation to a wedding. It's the opening of a gym. We're not going."

Instinctively Donna stiffened. "Maybe you're not going,

**37**

but my only daughter is being married (hallelujah!) for the first time and I'm not about to miss it. Tomorrow the bride's mother is going shopping for her outfit for the wedding, with or without the bride's father."

The next day, Donna looked at her reflection in the fitting room mirror. She had experienced dizziness in a fitting room on only one other occasion, and that was the day she tried on a bathing suit wearing knee-hi hose. Today was a close second. Plum tights that glowed from the strain of a million fat pockets of cellulite fighting to get out were covered by a pink leotard that rode high over the hips. A matching pink headband tried valiantly to keep her forehead from falling into her eyes. She looked at the leg warmers and prayed she wouldn't have a hot flash. She knew that if she so much as cleared her throat the crotch would bind her ankles together.

Poking her head outside the curtain, she said to the salesperson, "On second thought, I think the groom's mother is wearing this. I think I'll go for the blue velour warm-ups. A daughter only gets married (hallelujah!) once."

Her last stop was a sports center where a young man fitted her with running shoes. As she peeked into the X-ray machine to check the stress points on her new shoes, she asked, "By the way, young man, how far is 10 k's?"

"It's 6.2 miles," he said.

On the way home, Donna smiled to herself and mused, "He must have misunderstood. Probably thought I said Circle K."

Mel knew he was being stubborn, but he wasn't as forgiving of his daughter's independence and life-style as Donna. Around 8:30 PM on June 18, as he had done every five minutes that evening, he peeked through the Venetian blinds and spotted Donna emerging from a cab.

She limped noticeably while pressing her hand firmly on her backside.

"Where have you been?" he demanded.

"Oh Mel, you should have been there. It was wonderful. I started off at the park with everyone else and then I fought off three dogs, nursed two blisters, and finally hitched a ride with a motorcyclist who was going right by Jackie's Body Shop.

"Your daughter looked beautiful. They stood in front of a wall of mirrors and pledged to love one another forever as much as they did today, keep their bodies fit, and with God's love, both qualify for Boston with a 2:42.

"The groom's mother wore a T-shirt that read JOG-GERS DO IT BETTER and the minister had Band-Aids on his nipples to keep his shirt from irritating them as he ran.

"I ate a lot of health food, and met a lot of people—one woman who said her daughter was married in a free parachute fall over Omaha and had to pack her own parachute. We're having lunch next Tuesday. Just before Lynn left she took me aside and said if she continues to run thirty to forty miles a week she won't ovulate and so I shouldn't expect any grandchildren right away. She said that's the first meaningful conversation we ever had in our entire lives.

"Barry is built like the U.N. building and sells air conditioners at Sears. Oh, I was the only one there carrying a handbag, and I think I pulled a hamstring, but Mel . . . our daughter is . . . married!" (Hallelujah!)

**10**

# Hair

Every hundred years or so, the Earth shifts and goes into another cycle. I missed the Stone Age, the Ice Age, and the Glacial Period, but I was here for most of the Age of Hair.

It was the best of times and it was the worst of times.

Like most mothers, I devoted my life to the length of my son's hair. He would come down for breakfast and say, "Good morning," and I would reply "Get a haircut. One egg or two?"

We would be standing in church, and as the priest encouraged us to "extend to one another the sign of peace," I would turn to him, smile reverently, and say, "Get a haircut, weirdo."

It was all we ever talked about. We argued about barbers and the length of time between haircuts. We argued about the price of shampoo, the limitation of hot water, how he was screwing up our septic tank, and how we'd never unload him at the altar if he insisted on looking like Walter Matthau in drag.

He would come home and try to tell me the barber gave him a Timothy Leary trim.

"It looks more like a King Kong clip to me."

"What's a King Kong clip?"

"A light trim on your hands and ankles."

"There's no pleasing you," he shouted.

"Try!" I shouted back.

I always thought I was fair. I told him, "Hair can be as long, as shabby, and as dirty as it wants to be. It can be braided around the head five times or hang down to the tailbone in a ponytail . . . as long as it's on someone else's son."

The more I talked, the longer the hair became and the more fragile our relationship became.

In twelve years, not once did I give his hair a rest or miss an opportunity to harp on how he had disappointed me as a son.

Then one day he came into the kitchen and said, "When's dinner?"

I said mechanically, "You've got time to get a haircut. It's at 6:30."

He said, "Okay."

I nearly fainted.

When he returned, his hair was neatly trimmed and cleared his ears. We both smiled awkwardly. Like strangers on a blind date.

"So, what's been going on?" I asked.

"Not much," he stammered. "What about you?"

I had no idea what a large part of our relationship had been based on such intimacies as, "How long does it take you to wash that mop?" "How are you financing your shampoo these days?" "Did you know Attila the Hun once wore that style?"

There was absolutely no rapport between us. His hair had been the only thing that had kept us together . . . the only common ground of communication we had.

I began to remember the good times . . . the time we

ragged him about his hair on a vacation from Gary, Indiana, to Salt Lake City, Utah. The time really flew.

I recalled the time I told him I had enrolled him in a Miss Radial Tire competition and he had won.

Oh, I tried new lines of communication like, "You live like a hog," "There is no boy so tall as the one who stoops to pick up a towel," and "Don't ruin your dinner with that junk!" But somehow it wasn't the same.

We had lost that wonderful hostility that parents need to relate to their children.

Then one day he came home from school and my face lit up. "What's that disgusting bit of hair around your mouth and chin?"

"I'm growing a beard," he said.

"And sit at my table, you're not. I cannot believe that's the chin I used to spend hours wiping the saliva and oatmeal from. Why are you doing this to your mother?"

"I'll keep it trimmed."

"Hah. You show me a man with a beard and I'll show you what he had for lunch. It smells like pizza right now."

"All the influential men of the world have had beards, like Moses, Christ, and Burt Reynolds."

"You forgot King Henry VIII, Lenin, and Satan. I'll be honest with you. You look like one of the Seven Dwarfs."

"I knew you wouldn't understand," he said, slamming the door.

At least the beard would take us through Christmas vacation.

**11**

*What kind of a mother would ...*
**wash a measuring cup with soap after it only held water?**

# Sharon

Everyone said Sharon was a terrific mother.

Her neighbors said it.

She painted the inside of her garbage cans with enamel, grew her own vegetables, cut her own grass every week, made winter coats for the entire family from remnants, donated blood and baked Barbara Mandrell a doll cake for her birthday.

Her mother said it.

Sharon drove her to the doctor's when she had an appointment, color-coordinated the children's clothes and put them in labeled drawers, laundered aluminum foil and used it again, planned family reunions, wrote her Congressman, cut everyone's hair and knew her health insurance policy number by heart.

Her children's teacher said it.

She helped her children every night with their homework, delivered her son's paper route when it rained, packed nutritious lunches with little raised faces on the sandwiches, was homeroom mother, belonged to five car pools and once blew up 234 balloons by herself for the seventh grade cotillion.

Her husband said it.

Sharon washed the car when it rained, saved antifreeze from year to year, paid all the bills, arranged their social schedule, sprayed the garden for bugs, moved the hose during the summer, put the children on their backs at night to make sure they didn't sleep on their faces, and once found a twelve-dollar error in their favor on a tax return filed by H & R Block.

Her best friend said it.

Sharon built a bed out of scraps left over from the patio, crocheted a Santa Claus to cover the extra roll of toilet paper at Christmastime, washed fruit before her children ate it, learned to play the harpsichord, kept a Boston fern alive for a whole year, and when the group ate lunch out always figured out who owed what.

Her minister said it.

Sharon found time to read all the dirty books and campaign against them. She played the guitar at evening services. She corresponded with a poor family in Guatemala . . . in Spanish. She put together a cookbook to raise funds for a new coffee maker for the church. She collected door to door for all the health organizations.

Sharon was one of those women blessed with a knack for being organized. She planned a "theme party" for the dog's birthday, made her children elaborate Halloween costumes out of old grocery bags, and her knots came out just right on the shoelaces when they broke.

She put a basketball "hoop" over the clothes hamper as an incentive for good habits, started seedlings in a toilet paper spindle, and insulated their house with empty egg cartons, which everyone else threw away.

Sharon kept a schedule that would have brought any

other woman to her knees. Need twenty-five women to chaperone a party? Give the list to Sharon. Need a mother to convert the school library to the Dewey Decimal System? Call Sharon. Need someone to organize a block party, garage sale, or school festival? Get Sharon.

Sharon was a Super Mom!

Her gynecologist said it.

Her butcher said it.

Her tennis partner said it.

Her children . . .

Her children never said it.

They spent a lot of time with Rick's mother, who was always home and who ate cookies out of a box and played poker with them.

**12**

*What kind of a mother would...*
**lose her amateur status by turning pro?**

# Louise and Estelle

Next to hot chicken soup and vitamin C, Louise considered breakfast with her children as the most overrated ritual in American culture.

What was so great about sitting around a table with two surly kids fighting over fifteen boxes of unopened cereal?

She relented once a year. She called it her Annual Christmas Breakfast with Mommy, complete with candy canes and favors. The rest of the time Louise worked at staying out of their way.

She had discovered early that she was not like other mothers. It disgusted her to take knots out of shoelaces with her teeth that a child had wet on all day. She was bored out of her skull sitting around buying hotels for Park Place with funny money. She was not fulfilled walking around with a handbag full of used nose tissue handed her by her children to dispose of.

Housework didn't do a lot for her, either. Neither did the women who talked about it. She refused to break out in hives just because someone had found a way to get spaghetti stains out of plastic place mats. One day when the group was talking about Heloise's eighty-seven uses for nylon net, Louise snapped, "Why don't we just make butterfly nets out of it, throw it over ourselves, and check in at a home?"

Her goal in life was to hire a woman who would come in and sit with her children while she worked.

Her husband would not hear of it. "Give me a reason," he kept insisting.

"I'm bored," said Louise.

"That's not a reason," he said. "That's a symptom. You should keep busy."

Maybe he wanted her to lie like Elsie Waggoner, who said she got a part-time job to buy her daughter's Barbie and Ken dolls a wardrobe to go to Ohio State for the weekend.

In desperation, Louise did the next best thing. She volunteered.

It didn't take long for word to get out that Louise was "easy." She'd chair anything. She'd save animals she hadn't even heard of, raise funds for diseases she couldn't pronounce, and sit through three-hour meetings where the only decision made was where to have the next meeting.

In 1973 she set a record for volunteering more hours in a year than any other woman in the community.

She also set another record . . . unofficially. Louise hired and fired more babysitters in a year than any other woman in the history of women's liberation.

Louise demanded a woman who would read to her children and play games with them when they were bored.

She wanted a woman who would be there to share their day.

She wanted a woman who would bake them cookies, mend their broken toys, and kiss their scraped knees.

She wanted Julie Andrews flying around with an umbrella for a buck an hour.

The list of women who worked for Louise Concell would fill a book. There was Mrs. Crandel, who was a soap opera addict and between noon and 2 PM the world stopped.

There was Mrs. Sanchez, who made gin ice cubes and was discovered only when one of the children had a lemonade stand and every kid in the neighborhood slept through three meals.

Carol from the university lasted only a week, when the children began quoting from a Cheech and Chong album, causing Louise's teeth to go numb.

In the fall of 1979, Louise and her husband succumbed to temptation—a paying job that would take all her energies and time. She was chosen to serve as director of the Tinkerbell Child Care Center. Louise was ecstatic. She would have more responsibilities than she had ever had before, and for the first time there would be a price tag on her worth. She began a serious talent search for a surrogate Mother of the Year.

That's when she found Estelle. Estelle was too good to be true. She was young, had two children of her own, knew how to entertain them, feed them, and discipline them with firmness and love. She also drove.

Estelle had been a single parent for two years and had been through an entire alphabet of government services and organizations. At the moment, she was enrolled in the Social Awareness Program for Black Women that met in the church social hall every Wednesday.

She dropped her children, Glenn and Missy, off at the nursery in the room next door and took her place at a long table holding the Craft of the Day.

Today's project was simple enough. All she had to do was paint a cigar box and let it dry. Then take pieces of macaroni, dip them in paste, and place them on top of the cigar box. When it was completely covered, she sprinkled the entire box with sequins and, *voilá*, a jewelry box.

The only problem was she had no jewelry.

Estelle fingered the macaroni slowly and wondered about her life. What did she have to show for her two years at SAPFBW? A macramé pot. A crocheted Mexican hat that fit over a bottle of Tabasco sauce, a picture of an English cottage in bottle caps, and a piggy bank made out of a bleach bottle.

And now the pasta experience.

Angry with herself, she grabbed the bag of macaroni, took it home, cooked it and vowed to find a job.

Estelle loved her children and didn't want them to suffer for her restlessness. She had heard good things about the Tinkerbell Child Care Center.

"Do you have any questions about us?" asked Louise Concell. "After all, that's what I'm here for."

"Do you keep the children busy?" asked Estelle. "I mean, I don't want a place where they nap all day long."

"I think you'll find we have a superb activities program," said Louise.

"What about the teachers? My kids have never been away from me for any length of time."

"They love them as they do their own. Trust me," smiled Louise.

"I want someone around my children who doesn't consider it just a job but who really wants to be with them."

"I understand perfectly," said Louise, smiling. "We close at 6:15. Is that a problem?"

"Actually, I don't have a job yet," said Estelle. "I wanted to try the children out here while I start looking."

Louise pushed her glasses to the top of her head. "Have you thought of child care?"

Estelle shook her head.

"You see, I have two young children at home and I was looking for someone to sit with them. Do you mind if I ask you a few questions?"

"That's what I'm here for," said Estelle.

"I would want planned activities for the children so they're not watching the tube all day. They have such a low threshold of interest. You know, busy work."

"I've had plenty of experience with that in the last couple of years." Estelle smiled.

"My children would have to like you. You see, I've always been a mother who has stayed at home, and they're not used to being around anyone else."

"I've always been good with children. Trust me."

"This is difficult for me to explain," said Louise, "but my children have always been rather special to me and I don't want someone who is just being with them for money, but someone who really loves them and wants to be with them."

"I know where you're coming from," said Estelle.

So it was in September, 1980, both Louise and Estelle became "career mothers" . . . for minimum-wage scale.

They both wiped noses, changed diapers, rocked babies, hummed lullabies, and made bloody fingers well again with the touch of their lips.

Neither could explain why being paid for it made such a difference.

**13**

# How I Spent My Summer by Laura Parsons, Age 11

I spent my summer the same way I spent my winter. I'm a mini-mom. When my mom is away at work, I take care of my younger brother and three sisters.

A mini-mom's job is boring.

I take my brother and sisters to the bathroom when they don't want to go.

I wash their faces when they jerk their heads away.

I wipe their runny noses when they don't want them to be wiped.

I put them to bed when they're not sleepy.

And when they follow their "real mother," I grab them around the neck and hold on tight until they turn purple.

There is a lot of hitting and spitting with the job.

I wish I had never been born first. I thought it would be neat, but that's before I found out that I would be the first to reach the top shelf and have to get glasses down . . . the first to know how to button, tie and zip . . . the first one to be old.

I wish I could be a "sitter" instead of a mini-mom.

Sitters get neat snacks and tips if the house isn't wrecked. They get treated like a sister.

Mini-moms get blamed if someone turns the garden hose on in the living room and punished if someone eats the bananas mom was saving. We're treated like mothers.

Being a mother really grosses me out. I hate wiping someone after they go to the toilet. I hate it when I call a thousand times and they pretend they don't hear me. I hate not having any time to be by myself.

They like their real mom better than they like me. I don't care.

I wanted to run away from home, but my mother would kill me if I went out on the highway before they put a traffic light in.

I don't want to be a mother. Ever.

**14**

# The Five Greatest American Fiction Writers of All Time (Who Just Happen to Be Mothers)

## EILEEN WHORF
## (Author of the Poetry Club Letters)

September 16, 1978

Mrs. Loretta Flake
Bramblebush Acres
Norman, Oklahoma

My Dear Mrs. Flake:

      I cannot tell you how surprised and shocked I was to learn that I had been nominated to succeed you as president of the Walt Whitman Poetry Club.

      Especially since I attended only one of your meetings as a guest.

      Although I am honored to be considered, it is with great regret that I must decline to serve as your president next year.

      I know you will understand when I tell you I am terrified to get up before anyone to speak. It's a congenital shyness that I have learned to live with, but it certainly would not serve the best interests of the Walt Whitman Poetry Club.

Gratefully,

Eileen Whorf

September 21, 1978

Dear Loretta:

Thank you for your letter of insistence. I do agree that the more one speaks, the more comfortable one becomes. However, there is still another reason why I cannot serve as your president. I haven't told anyone (even my husband) about a small cyst on my right toe. It is probably benign, but we never know and I would not have your membership suffer because of my infirmity. I know you will keep my little secret.

Trustingly,

Eileen Whorf

September 26, 1978

Dear Loretta:

If perseverance were little drops of rain, you would have drowned weeks ago. I know I could count on the understanding and support of your membership, and thank you for reminding me of the Cyst Leave of Absence in the by-laws. However, there is a possibility that Mr. Whorf is being transferred to another country, in which case it would be impossible for me to commute to the monthly meetings of the Walt Whitman Poetry Club. Surely there is someone in your membership worthy of the honor you have tried to bestow on me with such force.

Regards,

Eileen Whorf

October 1, 1978

Dear Loretta:

You and your membership astound me with your generosity, and although I know you are willing to allow me to serve as your president until we move out of the country, there is still another reason.

I don't drive.

Anticipating your reply, I don't like to ride with anyone either.

Regards,

Eileen Whorf

October 4, 1978

Look, Loretta, I don't even know who Walt Whitman is!

Eileen Whorf

October 7, 1978

Loretta:

I accept.

Eileen Whorf
Reluctant President of
the Walt Whitman Poetry
Club

# BARFY WHITCOMB
## (Author of the annual Christmas Newsletter)

Christmas, 1982

Dear Friends and Relatives:

Heigh Ho, everyone.

Another year has gone by, and it's time to bring you up to date on the Whitcombs.

Our Lewiston took his college entrance exams and was accepted at Harvard. (Sob. Sob. Sixteen seems so young to go to school so far from home.) Bob and I will drive him to Boston, as he is talking about taking his Russian icon collection with him. (You can't tell children anything!)

As you can see by the enclosed picture, Melody has certainly filled out. She is following in her mother's footsteps at Seward High by being named head of the Pom and Flag drill team. The head of Pom and Flag is automatically named Prettiest Girl in the Class and Homecoming Princess at the Farewell Waltz. The theme this year is "Some Enchanted Evening." You're going to die, but that was exactly the same theme as the year I was Princess! Couldn't you scream?

Bob has had another promotion since last year's letter, putting us in another tax bracket (ugh). I am busy with my volunteer work. Last year I gave seventy-four phone hours to soliciting baked goods for the Bake-A-Rama. I was named Top Call Girl by the League.

In June, the Whitcombs "roughed it" on a camping venture. Imagine traveling six hundred miles with no Cuisinart! Our camper was forty-five feet long and Bob went crazy trying to back it into a spot in the campgrounds. Melody said it was what he got for not going where there was valet parking. Melody is a stitch. (Three of her quotes have been used by *Reader's Digest*.)

I must say it was a trip to remember. We saw a bird eating bread off a picnic table and one day visited a discount house. You have to admit, Barfy Whitcomb married adventure!

Tragedy struck the household in August. Chelsey, our prize-winning poodle, was raped by a German shepherd who forced his way in through the mail drop. No one fought harder for her honor than Bob.

Bob and I went to State for our twentieth reunion. You can imagine my shock when the usher directed us to the "student section." Everyone wanted to know what we did to stay so eternally young. We don't do anything special. We just eat properly, exercise regularly, and are rich.

I want to thank all of you who commented on last year's letter. (You know, the one where I paraphrased all the Whitcombs' achievements to "The Night Before Christmas.") It's gratifying to know that someone appreciates what it takes to get something to rhyme with "opulence."

Joyeux Noël
Feliz Navidad
Merry Christmas

Barfy and Bob
Melody and Lewiston
Chelsey and Bruno

# BILLIE
## (Author of letter to former classmate regarding impending visit)

April 12, 1982

Dear Sal:

What a surprise to hear from you. I can't believe it was three years ago since you and your family last visited. But then I counted back to when I got the sofa recovered and new mattresses (is Tommy toilet-trained yet?) and the car repainted, and you're right. Three uneventful years.

Since you are such a good friend, I know you will understand when I tell you we are sorry we are not going to be home when you pass through this time, even though you did not pin your visit down to a definite date. There are so many reasons, I hardly know where to begin.

First, Mother has become a problem. Whenever she has a "spell," we must run. I know this sounds vague and mysterious, but I'll explain later, when I have more time. It's sort of like your little Warren. Does he still love to watch fire?

Bill and I may go around the world all summer. Nothing definite. It's still in the planning stages and will depend on whether business picks up at the gas station and if he can get time off and we can scrape the money together and you know how it is.

If we stay home, we may paint the entire house inside and out, and you know what a mess that can be when you're visiting. (Especially if your Mona locks herself in the bathroom and mixes her "secret potion" in the toilet bowl.)

The children are also thinking of going to camp and it certainly wouldn't be any fun for your little cherubs to sit around with nothing to do. (Our Michelle still talks about your Myron using her for a dart board.)

I cannot believe there are so many circumstances converging to keep us apart. It was so hard to say good-bye to you the last time.

Please call us just before you come so I can bring you up to date on our plans.

Love,

Billie

P.S. We may be moving.

## GRACE REINGOLT
### (Author of letter to the president of Roy's Sonic TV and Appliance Center regarding broken handle on refrigerator door)

June 4, 1982

Dear Roy:

On March 21 of this year, for no reason, the handle of our refrigerator door fell off. Neither my husband Stoney nor I was in the room at the time.

We called you the morning of March 21, at which time your serviceman Duane came to check it out. He said there was no way the handle could have come off by itself, as the three-inch pin in it was bent double. Now I ask you, who do you think did it? Certainly not my husband or I, who were watching "Dukes of Hazzard," and certainly not our four-year-old son Budro, who was swinging from the spare tire in his bedroom at the time of this unfortunate event.

You have always been fair in the past. You may recall when a tube of toothpaste for no reason manifested itself in the lint trap of our dryer and a live dog wearing pantyhose wrapped around the pulsator in the washer, obviously there before it left the factory.

I suppose you are used to these apparitions, but to us they smack of poltergeist. Wishing to save you the trouble of replacing the handle, we have contacted our insurance company who said it would have to be an act of God in order to make a claim. (He obviously has never had an evening when he was separated from his gusto by a door without a handle!)

I am sad to report the warranty ran out on the refrigerator eighteen years ago next month. However, knowing how you want to protect your reputation for fairness, we look for an early settlement at no cost to us, the victims.

Regards,

Grace Reingolt

# MELISSA JOHNSEY
## (Author of advance instructions to her mother who will be babysitting Bo, her six-week-old daughter)

Mom—

Please have more light bulbs for changing crib and bumper pads before Bo arrives. Last time the supply was inadequate.

Have on hand four boxes of daytime diapers for a 15-pound infant.

One gallon skim milk. Make sure the date is recent for freshness.

Plenty of moisturized towels and plastic bags for dirty diapers.

Bottles can be washed in the dishwasher. However, nipples and caps must be done by hand. Push water through hole in nipple to make sure it works. Gas bubbles can be painful to an infant.

Phisoderm soap.

Vanilla ice cream.

Two plastic pails and a large basket for laundry. Commercial washer and dryer may be used.

No pets in room being occupied by the baby.

Phone must be off the hook while baby is sleeping.

Rectal thermometer should be shaken down after each use and stored in alcohol.

Do not place crib under duct.

Keep toys in plastic bag when not in use.

Sprinkle baby powder on hands and not directly on area to be powdered.

Be sure to put hand behind her head to support her.

Don't tickle, play hide-and-seek, or patty-cake in excess. Levity makes her spit up.

Check occasionally for fever. (Emergency numbers on separate sheet.)

It's your grandchild. Relax and enjoy her. The three hours will pass in no time.

Love,

Melissa

**15**

*What kind of a mother would . . .*
**die and not take you with her?**

# Julie

Had Julie not been the deceased, it was a funeral she would have loved.

The minister, in his desperate struggle for an analogy of comfort, said to her three sons sitting rigid in the front row, "Think of your mother as the spirit leaving the body. The shell is here, but the nut is gone."

The organist forgot the music and the only song she knew by heart was "Days of Wine and Roses."

And her middle son, Steve, flew in from school with only the shoes on his feet . . . a pair of red, white, and blue Adidas with stars that glowed in the dark, which he wore with a three-piece brown suit.

It was hard to believe Julie was dead at forty-eight, the victim of a "kind" cancer that acts quickly and with accuracy.

Chuck, the eldest, had been in his apartment when his grandmother called with the news. All he had been told until then was that his mother had been "a little tired lately."

She had been so proud of her son, "the television mogul." Actually, he was a prop man for a sitcom, but his degree had been in cinema and he spoke the language.

Every time they were together, he couldn't resist showing off. "What movies have you seen lately, Mom?"

JULIE: " 'The Seduction of Miss Marple' and I loved it . . ."
CHUCK: "It missed making a statement."
JULIE: "Up to a point. Of course, the one I really liked was 'Trilogy: Blood, Sex, and Violence.' It was breathtakingly . . . "
CHUCK: "Stargins had a concept. It just didn't work."
JULIE: "Dull. You're absolutely right. I thought 'Slime' was really gross . . ."
CHUCK: "Beautiful, sensitive film."
JULIE: ". . . grossed a million and was worth every penny."

How could he have been such a superior jerk? Now it was too late to say he was sorry. He had had no right to put her down. He fingered the letter in his pocket addressed to him in his mother's hand and opened it slowly. It was her last message to him. He unfolded the pages carefully as if to savor them.


Dearest Chuck:

Since this letter is for no one's eyes but yours, I can tell you that I always loved you best.

Maybe it was because you were the first miracle to stir inside me. The first hint of my immortality.

You were a part of the lean years for your father and me . . . the part that brought laughter to poverty, warmth to cold, success to failures.

You were the original model. There would be others who would come after you who might blow bigger air bubbles, burp louder, talk earlier, walk faster, or "go potty" sooner, but you did it first.

You may have suffered a bit from our inexperience with open pins, clumsy baths, and overprotection, but you got something better. You got our patience, our stamina, and our youth.

You got the part of us that was the best we had to give. Our struggle and our triumph over it. You were Hamburger Helper. You were redeeming bottles for movies. You were fresh grandparents who woke you up when you were asleep to rock you to sleep. You were six volumes of baby pictures and a set of encyclopedias. You were house calls for gas pains. You were strained lamb. You were the beginning. You were wanted and you were loved.

Mama

Chuck folded the letter quickly as Steve slid in beside him.

"Did you get a pen knife with those?" he snapped, nodding toward the red, white, and blue jogging shoes.

"No, a Frisbee."

Steve took a deep breath and tried to focus anywhere but on his brothers. He hadn't been able to look at Chuck since he had read the letter his mother sent him. He had never known she had felt that way about him or even why.

Steve had worked on being a maverick. Every time he screwed up, his mom always took him aside and said they understood, but they didn't. Not really. A couple of years ago, they took his other brother Tim to visit Chuck at school for a weekend and left him in charge of the house.

Why couldn't she have blown up like any other mother

would have? Instead, the night they returned, she said, "Want to tell me what happened?"

"What makes you think anything happened?" he asked.

"The thirty neighbors standing around in their night-clothes watching three police cruisers parked on our front lawn and the dog that is wearing my underwear. A lucky guess."

"I had a party."

"According to the police report you had a 746."

"What's a 746?"

"I'll read it to you. 'Blocking off street for a parade without permission. Illegal parking of two Porta-Johns on a carport, holding an assistant principal against his will, and unlawful assembly of 150 people in a house built as a single family dwelling.' "

Why had he been so stupid? All he had to say was "I'm sorry" and she'd have forgiven him, but he couldn't say it. Now he'd never get the chance. He felt the letter. It was still there. How could she have known him so well?

Dearest Steve:

You must have suspected, but I will say it anyway. I have always loved you best.

You drew such a stupid spot in the family and instead of caving in, you became all the stronger for it. How I did admire your fire, your independence, and your impatience. You may have worn faded, played with chipped toys, and never in your life did anything first, but you rose above it.

You are the child we relaxed with and enjoyed. The one who made us realize that a dog could kiss you on the mouth and you wouldn't die from it. If you missed a nap, you wouldn't get sick. If you sucked on a pacifier until age two, your teeth wouldn't grow in a circle.

## MOTHERHOOD: THE SECOND OLDEST PROFESSION

You were a part of our busy, ambitious years. The time when priorities and values can get so mixed up. But you reminded us of what we were all about and put us back on course when we strayed.

You were the sibling that unseated the only child. You were spaghetti and meatballs at eight months. You were checking accounts written down to twenty-seven cents. You were shared birthdays. You were arguments over bills. You were the new house we couldn't afford. You were staying home on Saturday nights. You took us away from tedium, rescued us from boredom, and stimulated us with your zest for life.

You were the constancy and were loved.

Mama

Tim stared at his brothers sitting with him in the pew. His suit was tight. At fourteen, it didn't take him long to outgrow anything.

He felt sorry for his brothers. They had missed a part of their mother that only he knew. When they lived at home, she gave and they took. For the last year Tim gave and she was helpless to do anything but accept. Thank goodness he had had that year to make up for all the grief he had given her.

He had hated being the "baby." He had hated the comparisons, the loneliness, the protectiveness, the references to "our second family." He lived in a house where all his parents did was diet and watch animal documentaries.

The only time he saw sugar was when his brothers came home for a visit. Then there was a lot of talk about "being a family again." What did they think he was? A computer?

His brothers had had it all. A father who played touch

football after dinner. A grandma who bought them digital watches for their 10th birthdays before she got "practical." A mother who had been too busy to alphabetize their baseball cards and put them in files.

Over the past year, they had talked out all the resentment inside him. The letter his mother had left said it all.

Dearest Tim:

A mother is not supposed to have favorites, but I have always loved you best.

Just when your father and I thought youth had left our lives, you came along to remind us we had something left to give. You darkened our hair, quickened our steps, squared our shoulders, restored our vision, revived our humor.

You were our second chance to enjoy a miracle from God.

You grew so fast in such a short time—or maybe it was that we didn't want to think about time. You fell heir to broken baseball bats, trains that wouldn't run, a refrigerator full of yogurt, midlife crises, and a baby book with nothing in it but a recipe for Apple Brown Betty.

You also fell heir to the one thing we never counted on: our mortality.

With you, we discarded the rules and experienced what a baby is all about. It was like seeing one for the very first time. It's a love one cannot describe.

I have loved you for your thirty-five-year-old patience, your ninety-year-old compassion, and your fifty-year-old practicality, but mostly, I love the fourteen-year-old boy who wore them awkwardly, but proudly.

You were the culmination and were loved.

Mama

As the last strains of "Days of Wine and Roses" faded, two women left from the back of the church.

"Didn't it just tear your heart out to see those young boys of hers without a mother?"

The other woman leaned closer and whispered, "I heard the medical bills took all they had. She didn't leave those boys a thing."

# ❦ 16

# The Special Mother

Most women become mothers by accident, some by choice, a few by social pressures, and a couple by habit.

This year, nearly 100,000 women will become mothers of handicapped children. Did you ever wonder how mothers of handicapped children are chosen?

Somehow, I visualize God hovering over Earth selecting His instruments for propagation with great care and deliberation. As He observes, He instructs His angels to make notes in a giant ledger.

"Armstrong, Beth, son. Patron saint, Matthew.

"Forest, Marjorie, daughter. Patron saint, Cecilia.

"Rutledge, Carrie, twins. Patron saint . . . give her Gerard. He's used to profanity."

Finally, He passes a name to an angel and smiles, "Give her a handicapped child."

70

The angel is curious. "Why this one, God? She's so happy."

"Exactly," smiles God. "Could I give a handicapped child a mother who does not know laughter? That would be cruel."

"But does she have patience?" asks the angel.

"I don't want her to have too much patience, or she will drown in a sea of self-pity and despair. Once the shock and resentment wear off, she'll handle it.

"I watched her today. She has that sense of self and independence that are so rare and so necessary in a mother. You see, the child I'm going to give her has his own world. She has to make it live in her world and that's not going to be easy."

"But Lord, I don't think she even believes in you."

God smiles. "No matter, I can fix that. This one is perfect. She has just enough selfishness."

The angel gasps. "Selfishness? Is that a virtue?"

God nods. "If she can't separate herself from the child occasionally, she'll never survive. Yes, here is a woman whom I will bless with a child less than perfect. She doesn't realize it yet, but she is to be envied.

"She will never take for granted a spoken word. She will never consider a step ordinary. When her child says 'Momma' for the first time, she will be witness to a miracle and know it. When she describes a tree or a sunset to her blind child, she will see it as few people ever see my creations.

"I will permit her to see clearly the things I see—ignorance, cruelty, prejudice—and allow her to rise above them. She will never be alone. I will be at her side every minute of every day of her life because she is doing my work as surely as she is here by my side."

"And what about her patron saint?" asks the angel, his pen poised in mid-air.

God smiles. "A mirror will suffice."

**17**

*What kind of a mother would...*

**get a sitter and go bowling on Mother's Day?**

# Ginny

The moment the dog started barking Ginny knew her sister was coming.

In seven years, he had tried without success to sink his teeth into her thighs, but Peggy's thighs were just too ambitious, even for a full-grown Doberman.

"That dog should be owned by an attorney," snapped Peggy. "You'd think in all these years he'd know I'm related. Where's B.J.?"

"Watching 'Days Of Our Lives.' "

"What could a fourteen-month-old baby get out of that?" she said sharply.

"A cheap thrill," sighed Ginny. "Nothing more."

Peggy shot her sister a look of disapproval and knelt down before the small child, who was propped up in a seat. "Hello, B.J.," she shouted. "It's Aunt Peggy. Remember Aunt Peggy? Of course you do."

"You don't have to shout," said Ginny. "He's retarded. Not deaf!"

Peggy slipped out of her coat. "You're not in another

one of your moods, are you? You look tired around the eyes."

"You want Brooke Shields? Come after lunch. Coffee?"

"Sure. Hold the sugar. I'm cutting back. Hey, did Sue call?"

"What's she selling?" snapped Ginny.

"What made you think she was selling anything? She just wants to invite us over for an evening of shallow conversation and a fattening dessert."

"Sue never serves cashews without a reason. She's always hustling something—plants, plastics, jewelry. Call me cautious, but I'm always suspicious when someone invites me over for dessert and then says, 'Oh by the way, wear clean underwear and bring your checkbook.' "

Peggy took her handbag off the table and hesitated. She didn't know if this was a good time or a bad time to give Ginny the column she had clipped from the newspaper on mothers of handicapped children.

She unfolded the column slowly. "Got something for you. As soon as I read it, I thought of you."

"Don't tell me. I've been named Miss Congeniality in the Pillsbury Bake-Off."

"I was going to save it for Mother's Day, but I think you need it today. Read it."

Ginny took a deep breath and began to read in a singsong voice. "Most women become mothers by accident, some by choice, a few by social pressures, and a couple by habit." Her head jerked up. "She forgot a bottle of Tequila in the back seat of a Toyota." She continued reading. "This year nearly 100,000 women will become mothers of handicapped children. Did you ever wonder how mothers of handicapped children are chosen?"

Ginny put the column down. "I'm throwing up already."

"Keep reading," Peggy ordered.

Ginny's eyes moved quickly across the lines without emotion. When she had finished reading the article, she threw it on the table and said, "It's crap."

"I thought you'd like it," sighed Peggy.

"Does she have a retarded child? Then who gives her the right to tell me how to feel? I'm sick of being patronized. It's tough enough having to deal with all this without someone trying to put a halo on me."

"I just thought . . ."

"This is reality," she interrupted. "Look at it. This is the only house on the block that will never have a swing set or a path across the yard. I'm a mother whose kid will never play in the toilet. Never tug at my leg when I'm on the phone. Never tear up my favorite magazine. Never run away from home stark naked. He'll never play patty-cake. Never pull my hair. He'll never even know my name."

"It sounds like you could use a night out. I'll sit if you want me to."

"I'm not looking for cute messages to stamp on tea towels. I'm madder than hell, don't you understand?"

"Don't you go to those meetings anymore?"

"What? Those group misery sessions where everyone sits around and tells you God never gives you more than you can handle? Well, I've got a flash. He overshot the field. I'm drowning, Peggy."

"You have to get out more."

"Don't you think I know that?" She sipped at her coffee. "I'm sorry, Peggy. It's just that I'm so scared. I can handle it now. I really can. Rob has been great. And Mom and Dad have been wonderful. Sometimes I forget how disappointed they must have been. But I'm worried about the long haul. I know what B.J. will be like ten years from now, but what will I be like? I don't like what bitterness does to people. I just want to be special to someone. Look, I didn't mean to take off, but every time I read something like this—"

"I understand," said Peggy, getting up. "Listen, I only stopped by for a minute. Need anything?"

Ginny shook her head and saw her sister to the door. "I'm sorry. Come back when I'm a human being." They put their arms around one another.

After Peggy left, Ginny looked at B.J. He sat quietly as "Days Of Our Lives" told a sensual story of greed, avarice, and carnal pleasures. Ginny stooped and wiped off his face with a piece of tissue, then stuffed it up her sleeve. "Well, what'll we do today, Tiger, play indoor volleyball?"

As she stood up, she caught her reflection in the mirror and paused for a closer look. She was stunned by what she saw. A thirty-year-old woman with hundred-year-old eyes. Eyes that were dull and listless. Eyes that held no joy. Eyes that looked but never seemed to see anything that interested them. Eyes that reflected no life—only pain.

Quickly, she turned away from the mirror and gathered up the coffee cups. Her eyes caught the phrase on the clipping, "When her child says 'Momma' for the first time, she will be witness to a miracle and know it."

She knelt beside B.J. "Look, B.J., there's something I've got to tell you. I'm no saint. It's important to me for you to know that. I have cursed you for my guilt, my exhaustion, and my life. I have questioned why both of us were born. I haven't figured out yet why He brought us together. I only know there is something special between us, something I can't even explain to Rob. I couldn't bear it if you were not here, or if you had never been.

**76**

"In the mirror just now I saw myself as you must see me—beaten and angry. I'm not like that. Honest. Sometimes, I think I'm the one who's handicapped." Ginny eased B.J. out of his sling chair and held him close as they both looked into the mirror.

"B.J., I've never made any demands on you. I've never asked you for anything, but right now, I want you to say 'Mama.' I know it's not going to be perfect, but try. Just make a sound. Grunt. Burp. Anything!"

The saliva came out of the corner of B.J.'s mouth. No sound came forth. Then Ginny noticed his eyes. They stared back into hers in a way she had never seen before. They didn't focus right away, then they looked at her for the first time. There was awareness in them, interest, recognition. He knew who she was!

Rob wouldn't believe her. No one would, but B.J. had just spoken his first word with his eyes. He had called her "Mama."

There were tears in her eyes. She took the article and shoved it into the stove drawer. It was still crap, but there *was* something to that miracle part.

# ♣ 18

# ¿Se Habla English?

When my son entered the first grade, his teacher asked to see me. She began our meeting by telling me, "He verbalizes during class, periodically engages in excursions up and down the aisle, has no viable goals and seemingly no definitive conception of his role expectations. Peer pressure seems advised at this time."

"Are you trying to tell me my son is goofing off?"

"I would not have expressed it in the vernacular, but you are correct."

When he was in the third grade, a teacher at open house opened his folder and announced, "To categorize the problem as simply as I know how, your son has challenged group management techniques, our academic expectations, and our sense of efficacy with his declining attention span, which at this time does not occupy a position of priority."

I took a shot and figured he was goofing off.

In the fourth grade he was still goofing off, but he was described as "lacking the basic skills of competency and languishing in his academic environment, even though he has not attained his cognitive limits."

In the sixth grade, I had a long talk with his teacher,

who said, "Your son has potential, but is incapable of any viable feedback. You tell me—what are we to do with a child who does not engage in social interaction, does not respond positively to established concepts, and persists in interruptive behavior? I'm sorry to come down so hard, but certainly you can understand the ills and lacunae of contemporary education."

I didn't even understand good-bye.

In the eighth grade, my husband answered the phone one night and did a lot of nodding. When he hung up, he turned to me and said, "Guess what? Our son is not motivated by curriculum innovation. They're apprehensive about his stagnating in a lock-step system, and they're trying to stimulate his awareness. What do you think it means?"

"I think it means he's goofing off."

He was in his sophomore year when he was diagnosed as "having problems that indicate behavior modification, perhaps in a modular-flexible schedule on which an aggressive monopolizer would diminish his role and force him to accept a lesser role in a nonpunitive, restraining, yet pleasant way."

At the beginning of his senior year, my son's adviser summoned me to her office and said, "Well, it's that time when we have to consider the conundrum, isn't it?" She laughed so I laughed too.

"It's hard to say where the burden for the lack of motivation and apathy lies, but before your son's achievement levels polarize, I thought we should have a little talk.

"Hopefully we can open options so he can realize his potential and aim for some tangible goals. Although accreditation is near at hand, I wanted to emphasize his need for upward mobility if he is to succeed on a postgraduate level."

On the way out, I leaned over to the secretary and said, "English! Do you speak English?"

She nodded.

"What was she talking about?"

"Your son is goofing off," she said flatly.

I don't know if education has helped my son or not, but it has certainly improved my vocabulary.

**19**

*What kind of a mother would...*
**hang up on E.T.?**

# Dottie

Dottie Fedstrom was a no-nonsense mother who raised her children by the rules.

Dottie Fedstrom made the Marine Corps look like an exercise in Show and Tell.

She was born to mother. She had hands like thermometers, two sets of eyes that could look through doors and tell at a glance when a child was constipated or lying. She had a nose that could smell chocolate on the breath of a child in another state with his head buried in a pillow.

Dottie had six daughters. She called them The Gang. She bought them white socks (one size fits all) and brown oxfords which were passed down from one sister to the next. Once she bought two bolts of navy corduroy and made each of them a jumper and had enough left over to make drapes and spreads for their bedrooms. (As one of her daughters observed, if you didn't smile, she wouldn't know if you were in your room or not.)

If one daughter wanted oatmeal for breakfast, they all got oatmeal. If one got the measles, Dottie made sure they all got them. If the first to get a watch lost hers, then none of the others would be trusted with one.

Whether they were twenty or two, they all had the same curfew and the same allowance, and got the same doll, the same sweater, album, and hair dryer for Christmas. Dottie didn't play favorites.

It surprised no one when the girls married young. They were as predictable as their mother. Eventually, Dottie was down to one daughter, Nicky.

For three years Nicky heard:

"I don't know why you don't let your hair grow like your sister Leslie's. You'd look good in that style instead of looking like a twelve-year-old boy."

"When Pammie had your room, she had that real pretty pink spread. I think it's still around here somewhere. I'm going to dig it out for you."

"Does your teacher know you're Wendy's sister? She should have recognized the dress. It was Wendy's favorite."

"You're exactly like your sister Leah. She never could manage her money either. Every week she wanted an advance on her allowance."

"You and Alice were never good judges of character."

"You'd better snap it up. All five of your sisters were married before their twenty-first birthday."

Nicky was destined never to do anything original in her entire life. She had been sired by a Xerox machine set for six copies.

Her wedding was predictable—a carbon copy of her sisters'. The dress was the same design; the flowers came from the same florist, the food was from the same caterers, the cake from the same bakery. She received from her parents the same gift her sisters had received: a toaster oven and two goose-down pillows.

As she waited in the small room at the back of the church before going down the aisle, her mother appeared with the same tearful face she had displayed at the weddings of her sisters. She cupped Nicky's face in her hands and whispered her last piece of advice (which had also been given to Nicky's predecessors): "Be yourself or you'll never find happiness."

# 🌼 20

# Two Be or Not Two Be

GRAND RAPIDS, MICH.—Robin Hawkins could be the little girl they had in mind when they named it the "terrible twos": the toddler has, by actual count, racked up nearly $3,000 in damages in two months.

First, it was the plumbing, then the dishwasher, the refrigerator, and the family car. None has escaped the $2,862 rampage of Rowlf and Bernie Hawkins' two-year-old daughter.

Robin's trail of terror began at the toilet, a familiar trouble spot for toddlers. A stuffed animal, named Alice the cat, got dunked, drowned, and flushed.

Hawkins, who dutifully has kept track of Robin's exploits, neatly tallied the expenses in a yellow tablet: $62.75 for the plumber, $2.50 for Alice.

That was only the beginning.

Robin's decision to give Teddy Bear a bath—atop the heating element in the dishwasher—cost her father $375 for repairs, $25 for smoke damage and, of course, $8 for the teddy bear.

Then there was the refrigerator. It seems Robin stuck

some magnetic letters in the vents just before the family left home for the weekend, burning out the motor. The cost: $310 for the refrigerator, $120 in spoiled food and $3.75 for the magnetic letters.

"That evening, we sat down to watch TV," said Hawkins, an East Grand Rapids police officer. "Robin had twisted the fine tune so far that it broke inside."

The repair bill: $115.

The next day, Mrs. Hawkins went to pick up her husband from his second job as a part-time officer in Sparta. She left Robin sleeping in her safety seat, with the keys in her purse inside the car.

"We heard the car start up, and we ran outside just in time to watch the car start down the street," Hawkins said.

The car ran into a tree. Cost: $1,029.52 in repairs.

A few days later, Robin tried to play some tapes in the family stereo. Cost: $36 for tapes and $35 for tape-deck repairs.

Shortly after that, the Hawkins (sic) parked their car halfway in the garage after a shopping trip and, because they were planning to unload groceries, decided to leave Robin strapped in her safety seat.

"My wife had the keys, so figured everything was OK," Hawkins said.

Everything was OK, until they heard a loud noise and went outside to find the automatic garage door bouncing off the hood of the car with—guess who?—locked inside the car, pushing the remote control. The bill: $120.

Robin also lifted $620 out of the cash register at a supermarket, drilled fifty holes in the walls of a rental property owned by her parents, painted walls with nail polish and slipped the garden tractor out of gear so it rolled down the driveway narrowly missing a neighbor out on a walk.

"Some day, when she comes and asks me why she isn't getting any allowance, I'll show her this," Hawkins said, waving the yellow pad containing an itemized list of his daughter's damages.

**21**

*What kind of a mother would . . .*
**buy vanilla a fifth at a time?**

# Brooke

Every time Brooke visited her sister, she never sat down without first running her hand over the chair.

The whole house was like a giant playpen inhabited by five active children with sticky hands, pacifier lips, and something running from every opening in their faces.

The house was a dump! A lone goldfish swam around in an Old Fashioned glass, the three silver iced tea spoons she'd gotten her in her pattern for her anniversary were stuck in the flower bed, and she could have sworn she saw a rainbow over the baby's diaper.

Both of them had been raised in an atmosphere of fine china, good books, oriental carpets, and cloth napkins. Somewhere, her sister had lost her way.

In six years of marriage, Brooke and her husband Clay had done a lot of thinking about how their child would be raised. Like every stick of furniture in their white and chrome townhouse, their two-seater sportscar, their his-and-her careers, and their club membership, their baby was planned.

Brooke would conceive in February, after the holiday parties were over, still be slim enough in May to work on her tan, and deliver in time to have the family portrait taken for the Christmas card.

Brooke and Clay made only one mistake.

They made promises to each other that new parents should never make:

Their baby would *not* dominate their lives.

They would never stoop to plastic.

They would never put their coffee-table books or art glass out of the reach of their child.

They would be able to take their child anywhere and not be embarrassed.

They said all of this in public where people could hear them.

Somewhere it is written that parents who are critical of other people's children and publicly admit they can do better are asking for it.

Other self-righteous people who have defied this law have included: Mia Farrow, who was delivered of "Rosemary's Baby," Lee Remick, who birthed Damien in "The Omen," and the parents of Lizzie Borden.

It came as no surprise to anyone except Brooke when she went into labor a month early at the Halloween party at the club and was rushed to the hospital where she gave birth to Wesley.

Her timing was lousy. She had gone to the party dressed as a nun.

Brooke stubbornly insisted Wesley wasn't a bad little boy, he was just "accident prone." He started each day like one of those battery-driven cars that you put on a track and it doesn't stop until it hits something and self-destructs. Brooke was fond of capping each trauma with, "Wesley is just 'all boy.' "

By the time Wesley was six, his medical charts read

like the first eighteen chapters of a first-aid manual. He drank paint tint and urinated Melody Blue for a week. He pulled a bubble gum dispenser on himself, fell out of his crib, swallowed a penny, cut his lip on a waste can, got his foot caught in a shopping cart and had to be torched out of it, ate a plastic banana, and bit a rectal thermometer in half.

He gouged himself in the eye with his own finger, broke his arm while watching TV, was bitten by a hostile turtle, fell on the ice and caused a boil on his tailbone, forced a golf tee in his ear, and made a bet he could swan-dive into two and a half feet of water, and lost.

Brooke made so many trips to her local emergency ward, they sent her cards when Wesley was well.

Through it all, never once did Brooke publicly admit defeat. Other children could watch TV and "waste time." Wesley could do it and be "curious and searching." Other kids could shove people out of the way and be "aggressive." Wesley could do it and be "ambitious." When other children took money from their mother's purse without her permission it could be construed as "stealing," but when Wesley did it, it was "reinforcement of the mutual trust between them."

Early in June, Brooke smiled stoically when her obstetrician told her the scanner revealed she was carrying twins.

Normally, that kind of news would have given a mother pause for reflection, but not Brooke.

She stopped on her way home to buy fresh flowers for the table.

She called her husband to tell him the news and thanked goodness the silver pattern of the baby spoon was open stock.

She called her sister to tell her their season opera tickets were still intact, even if the babies came early.

She told Wesley the news and sent him to the neighbors to play.

She retired to her room with a bottle of vodka and was not seen until 4 PM the next day.

**22**

# Born to Crisis

Some mothers are born to crisis.

They're ready for it. They sit around in color-coordinated outfits, with their car keys in one hand and a first-aid manual with illustrations of pressure points and CPR in the other.

When a child comes screaming in the back door, "Mommy! Mommy! Mikey has a bloody boo boo," this mother calmly instructs her oven to cook the dinner by six, backs the car (filled with gas) out of the garage, and off they go to the hospital.

She's always at the reception desk when I arrive with my child, who is wrapped in a dirty dish towel and wearing a pair of pajamas that I was going to use for a dust rag as soon as I ripped the snaps out.

She rattles off her insurance number by memory as I wrestle with my child's name and age, finally pinning his birth down to the year we paid off the freezer.

As she quietly goes to the waiting room holding the *Saturday Review of Literature* under her arm, I am checking every phone return for a dime to call my husband, Whatshisname.

One of the most difficult jobs of child-raising is knowing when your child needs medical attention and when he doesn't. Or as we say at the wine-tasting parties, "Be not the first on your block to race a case of constipation to the hospital, nor the last to call the pharmacist for a compound fracture."

There is possibly no guilt in this world to compare with leaving a sick child with a babysitter. The sitter could be Mother Teresa and you would still feel rotten. There is something about having your child throw up without you that is difficult to live with.

I once spent more time writing a note of instructions to a babysitter than I did on my first book.

Dear Miss Tibbles:

The suppositories are in the refrigerator next to the meal worms. The meal worms are for the lizard, who eats breakfast when everyone else eats breakfast. The suppositories are for Bruce's nausea. He will work against you, but persevere. Please return them to the fridge as they are better chilled. The antibiotic is to be given every 12 hours. Bruce is crabby at the 3 AM medication and he will spit it in your face, but remind him it is for his own good. Be firm! The baby aspirin are in the medicine chest on the top shelf. Start early, as the cap is childproof and difficult to remove. Simply depress the cap and twist at the same time in a counterclockwise movement until the arrow reaches the indentation and then, using your thumbnail, flip up. If you cannot get it off, give it to Bruce. He can whip that sucker off in two seconds flat.

He has not been able to tolerate solids yet, but try him on some gelatin and crackers. If he throws up, stop feeding him solids.

Mrs. Bombeck

Pediatricians are no help. Year after year, they dole out instructions that are some of the best comedy material being written today.

"Make sure he keeps it down" is a classic. And how about "Don't let him scratch." (That's like telling the Pope to buy a leisure suit.)

"Keep him quiet and in bed" is another goodie, but my all-time favorite is "Watch his stool."

Do you know of any mothers personally who have ever followed that advice? My son swallowed a nickel once. I was ready to declare it a tax write-off and forget it. My mother was outraged. "You have to take that child to a doctor and see where it is lodged. It could be serious."

The doctor examined him and through X-rays discovered the nickel had "traveled." He then turned to me and with a serious face said, "Watch his stool."

"Why would I want to do that?" I asked.

"For the nickel."

"Money is no object to us. We own our own home and have a microwave oven."

"It's not the money," he said. "Don't you want to know what happens to it?"

"Not that badly," I said.

There are some things you just don't ask a high school graduate to do.

**23**

*What kind of a mother would . . .*
**have her maternity clothes bronzed?**

# Cora

Cora is an important character in this book. Mostly because adults do a lot of kidding about children.

Complaining is a mother's escape hatch. That's why you hear a lot of, "Go out and play in the traffic" or "Marrying your father was my first mistake. You were my second." And on a bad day, "If God had meant for me to take you to church, He would have put restrooms at the end of each pew."

It's important that you meet Cora in the examination room at her gynecologist's. There's always something intimidating about the place.

Maybe it's because you're sitting in a chilled room in a paper dress (you've set drinks on a bigger piece of paper) waiting to discuss intimate things with a man who is two years younger than your cookie sheet.

On this day Cora cleared her throat and wished her feet looked better. The heels were cracked and her toenails needed cutting. She wished her whole body looked better. Since she stopped smoking six months ago, her body looked like an avocado. Even when she sucked in her stomach, nothing moved. Maybe he could give her a diet.

She reasoned she was stupid to come. There probably was nothing wrong with her. She was just tired. And probably ready for the estrogen connection.

The examination lasted less than three minutes and after a couple of questions and a few notations, the doctor smiled and said, "Congratulations: you're going to become a mother."

Cora looked him in the eye for the first time since he came into the room. "I'm going to become a what?"

"Mother," he said. "As in Teresa, McCree, and Nature."

She threw her arms around his neck and for a reason that made no sense to either of them, said, "Thank you!"

Cora couldn't believe it. For years she and Warren had tried everything. They had kept charts, burned candles, sought adoption, and even gone into debt (which everyone said was a sure-fire way to get pregnant). Nothing. Motherhood eluded her.

"You know I'm thirty-eight," said Cora, anxiously.

The doctor was without expression. "If you'd waited another year, the birth could have been covered by Medicare, not to mention *The New York Times*. Your uterus is tilted, so we're going to take some precautions."

Eleven weeks into her pregnancy, Cora climbed into bed and remained there until the birth of the baby six months later.

She ate her meals from a tray that Warren prepared every morning, watched soaps and game shows, read, and entertained the parade of soothsayers who wanted to relieve her of her happiness.

Her mother said, "Tell me again. What happened?"

Her sister-in-law said, "Are you aware the kid will take your social security card for Show and Tell?"

Her husband offered to lace her bran with Valium.

Her neighbor warned she'd feel different when the kid sat around connecting liver spots on Mommy's arms.

Her paper boy said, "I thought you were the oldest mother in North America, but I looked it up in the *Guinness Book of World Records* and there was a woman who gave birth when she was 57 years and 129 days."

Her former boss told her that the expression, "Children keep you young," was first said by a nineteen-year-old mother in Milwaukee who denied saying it when she turned twenty-two.

Somewhere in this chapter it should be said that most children are wanted. For every child abandoned in a bus station, there's a list of adoptive parents who have waited and prayed for years to hold a baby.

For every woman who has an abortion there are women who are fighting for both of their lives against stiff odds.

For every mother who complains how much a child costs, how much trouble they are, and how much different their lives would have been without them, there are thousands of women who would not have been whole without them.

In May, Cora delivered a healthy six-pound, five-ounce son. She had never known before, nor would ever know again, such a feeling of exhilaration.

There is a lot of Cora in most of us. More than we like to admit. At whatever age, we are awed by the miracle that stirs inside us. We are filled with joy and wonder by the process that gives us our immortality. Why are we so reluctant to admit it?

**24**

# Stepmothers with Bad P. R.

## SNOW WHITE'S STEPMOTHER

It was Queenie White's first marriage.

At thirty-seven, it was something she thought would never happen. Sometimes she had to pinch herself to make sure it wasn't a dream. She was married to a successful king, with a castle in the suburbs and a small beautiful child who looked like something out of a Pampers ad.

It should have been idyllic, but it wasn't. Snow resented her for marrying her father. Why couldn't it have been just the two of them? They were happy before she came along. At the wedding Snow had informed her new stepmother that she was wearing something old, something new, something borrowed, something blue. The symbolism was all wrapped up in one garment—a pair of raggy, faded jeans.

Queenie knew Snow was spoiled, but she was resigned to patience and never burdened her husband with the problem.

When Snow gave a slumber party at the castle for the jousting team, she covered for her. She took the blame for the dent in the King's carriage. She kept silent when she saw Snow and some friends smoking the croquet lawn.

One day she looked at her image in the mirror and said aloud, "Mirror, mirror on the wall, who's the stupidest of them all?" Before the mirror opened its mouth, she knew the answer.

Things couldn't continue. She dropped by Snow's room.

"Snow," she said softly, "we're not close and I don't know why."

"Because you're heartless and cruel," said Snow. "And you wish I'd split because I'm a constant reminder of how beautiful my mother was."

"I'd like for us to get along because we both love the same man and he deserves better," said Queenie.

"Stick it in your mirror," said Snow. "You think I haven't caught you carrying on a conversation with it? You're weird!"

"Do you have any idea what love really is? It's caring enough to tell you the truth even at the risk of losing your love. Why don't you get your act together? Stop dressing like trick or treat. Get some order to your life. Enroll at junior college. Volunteer. Or I'll tell your father what you've been up to."

That night, fearful that Queenie would make good her threat, Snow headed for the forest outside of San Francisco. She spotted a small cabin in the clearing, occupied by a commune. It was the first time she had ever checked in anywhere without a reservation. For the next three years, Snow played the guitar, grew her own vegetables, and made owl macramé planters for a local florist.

There is probably no guilt in this world to compare with that of a stepmother who has driven a child away from the family hearth. Queenie tried daily to find her.

Then one day a courier brought word from Snow.

Queenie duly reported it to her husband.

"We've found Snow."

"That's wonderful," said the King.

"Not so wonderful," said Queenie. "She's living in the forest in a commune."

"So, it could be worse. She could be living with a man."

"She's living with seven of them. All dwarfs."

"I want her home," said the King.

Snow returned with a husband, a baby, and asked to be reinstated in the family.

The couple and their child slept on mattresses surrounded by candles in sand, drank goat's milk, and ate sunflower seeds. They meditated and chanted all day long.

Queenie stood in front of the mirror one day and said, "Mirror, mirror on the wall, what must I do to survive it all?"

And the mirror answered, "Drink!"


## CINDERELLA'S STEPMOTHER

Her name was Buffy Holtzinger.

But to the world of fairy tales, she was identified only as "Cinderella's mean, evil, ugly stepmother."

Buffy attracted losers like a white dress attracts spots. First there was Ray, who left her high and dry with one small daughter and another on the way. And then there was Eugene, who brought his daughter, Cinderella, to the marriage, then split to get in touch with his feelings.

Buffy was one of the first working mothers in her

neighborhood. She held no illusions that she was a "real" mother (a fact which Cinderella reminded her of at least fifteen times a day). She worked. She came home. She shouted until she had varicose veins of the neck. She fell into bed. There was no doubt in her mind that if she continued raising three teenaged girls by herself she'd end up like Rapunzel sitting in a tower braiding her hair. She had to get them married off if she were to survive.

Her two natural daughters were bad enough. They were surly. They lounged around the house all day reading the *Palace Enquirer* (a gossip rag) and waiting for someone to spoon-feed them.

Goofing off Buffy could handle. But it was Cinderella's active imagination that drove her up the wall. From the beginning, Cinderella played with the truth like most kids play with their gum—stretching it, rearranging it, hiding it, and disguising it. She told her teacher in the third grade that her "stepmother" made her play outside naked in the snow. She told them her stepsisters got silk dresses for Christmas and she got a certificate to be "bled." She told everyone her stepmother hated her because she was pretty and made her wax the driveway.

One night, when Buffy was needlepointing a sampler that said, "YOU HAVE TO KISS A LOT OF TOADS BEFORE YOU FIND YOUR PRINCE," she summoned Cinderella to talk.

"Cinderella, why do you say things that aren't true?"

"I don't," said Cinderella defensively. "I do everything around here. I'm nothing but a slave. You like your kids better than you like me. Daddy and I were happy before you came along. If he were here, things would be different."

"All of us have chores," said Buffy tiredly. "And if all of you get them done you can go to the ball next Friday night. How would you like that?"

"Who are we kidding here?" snapped Cinderella, as she headed for the door. "You'll think of something to chicken out. The pots won't be sparkling enough or the floor won't shine enough. I hate you and I hate your stupid warts!"

"They're not warts! They're moles!" shouted Buffy after her.

The next Friday was predictable. Buffy's two older daughters made a stab at finishing their chores, but Cinderella was doing her Butterfly McQueen number. She flicked a speck of dust off with her finger, blew on it, and went on to the next brick.

Buffy called her bluff. "That's it! I made a rule and I'm going to hold you to it. You're grounded."

Several hours later no one was more shocked to see Cinderella at the ball than Buffy. She grabbed one of her daughters and said, "How did she get here?"

She popped another cheese puff into her fat cheeks. "She's telling everyone a fairy godmother made a coach out of a pumpkin, a coachman out of a white rat, footmen out of lizards, and horses out of frightened mice."

"Oh God," moaned Buffy. "Tell me she didn't say that to the reporter from the *Palace Enquirer*. They're going to put her away in a ha ha house. You tell her to get herself home or she won't be able to sit down for a wcck."

Cinderella met a shoe salesman that night at the ball and married him several months later. Happiness continued to elude Buffy when Cinderella submitted a manuscript to a publisher called *Stepmommie Dearest*. The title was changed to *Cinderella* and the book became an instant best seller.

It is credited with saving millions of women from a second marriage who are now living happily ever after.

# HANSEL AND GRETEL'S STEPMOTHER

Wilma met Hansel and Gretel's father at a wood-cutters' convention and it was magic. They liked the same music, the same food, and the same jokes. No one was surprised when, three days later, Wilma gave up her job as a secretary to marry Herb and go live with him and his two children in the forest.

From the beginning, Wilma sensed that the children resented her presence. They set the table for three. They coughed on her porridge so she couldn't eat it. And one night they put a dead wolf in her bed.

"Maybe they're getting too much sugar," she suggested to Herb. "They seem so hyper."

"Nonsense," he said. "They're just active little children. Try to have a little fun with them."

Wilma tried. She took them on picnics and they tied her to a tree. She read them little stories and they put a candle under her dress. Finally, Wilma faced the problem realistically. They were the type of children who would kill both parents and make you feel sorry for them because they were orphans.

When she told Herb that something had to be done about their behavior, he said, "So, what's your solution?"

"I think we should take them out into the forest and dump them." Seeing the horrified look on his face, she said, "I'm only kidding, Herb. Can't you take a joke?"

But just at that moment, a plan began to form in the warped little minds of Hansel and Gretel . . . a plan to get Wilma out of their lives for good. They planned an outing in the forest where they purposely got lost. When they returned, they told their father Wilma tried to ditch them. The only way they had found their way back was by dropping crumbs. "She's never liked us," said Hansel.

"Things were wonderful before she came," said Gretel.

The next week, they once again planned an outing with their stepmother, and this time disappeared forever, sealing Wilma's fate.

Several days after their disappearance, the little cottage was overrun with authorities taking fingerprints, looking for clues, and questioning Wilma and Herb until they were incoherent.

"There was a Rosemary's Baby quality about those two," said Wilma. "Something I couldn't put my finger on."

"They were just active little children," Herb growled.

"You weren't here the day they strapped 138 pigeons to their arms and said they were going to fly to South America," said Wilma. "I'm telling you, Herb, those kids were weird."

"Are you saying you're glad they're gone?" asked the inspector.

"I'm saying I think they planned to run away," said Wilma.

"Then why did we find crumbs of bread a few feet from the house? Is that the act of children who want to stay lost?"

Wilma had no answer. The case against her was too strong for her defense. She was a stepmother who had never displayed any real affection for her two charges. At one point during the trial, when someone mentioned that these two little children would never be seen again, Wilma laughed uncontrollably.

She was sentenced to life in prison for the questionable demise of two small innocent, helpless children.

Wilma was considered quite mad by those around her and incapable of communication. However, one day in the prison library, Wilma's eyes caught sight of a small story on an inside page of *The New York Times*. It seemed that two small children were being sought for shoving an old woman into an oven. They had conned their way into her home by telling her they had been abandoned in the forest by a wicked stepmother. After they did the old lady in, they ripped off all her treasures and escaped on the back of a white duck.

A chill went through Wilma's body. She wanted to stay where she was forever. She felt safe there.

**25**

*What kind of a mother would...*

**go in search of her daughter's "real mother"?**

Pat

So you're Joanie's "real mother."

I've made a million speeches to you in the bathroom mirror. They were all brilliant.

I thought you'd be taller. You always seemed taller when we talked about you. And you always looked like Barbara Stanwyck to me. Don't ask why.

We've talked about you a lot. As soon as Joanie— that's your daughter's name now—was able to focus, we told her she was adopted. We told her her real mother loved her so much that she was unselfish enough to give her up to someone who could give her all the things she couldn't. That's true, isn't it? No, never mind. I don't want to know.

Forgive me for staring. It's just that all my life, I've wanted to see what a "real" mother really looks like. Joanie always seemed to know you better than we did. You know, "My *real* mother wouldn't have done that" or "My *real* mother wouldn't have said that." That kind of thing.

I guess first off I should thank you for giving birth to

our child. I don't know how we would have gotten through life without Joanie. Children make your life important.

There's probably a lot of things you want to know about Joanie. Is she beautiful? Is she smart? Is she happy? Does she play the piano? I guess I owe you that.

It's funny. I've always wondered about my debt to you. Things like how *much* do I owe you? When is the debt paid? And when do I become "real"?

It's only fair that if you hear all the good stuff, maybe you have to hear the bad stuff. There were bad times, you know. Did you know that our—your—daughter almost died from an asthma attack when she was eight? I thought about you that night as both of us gasped for every breath together under that vaporizing tent. I said to myself, "Where in the hell are you now, *real* mother?"

Why am I doing this? Why am I so angry at you? I've always known you did what you thought was best. I can tell by the look on your face that you honestly don't know what you did that I think is so terrible.

I'm not sure myself. I only know that when you went away you took a part of our child with you that we can't give her. You took away her history!

Without a past, she's been adrift on a sea of frustration, sometimes afloat and sometimes sinking, and she doesn't even know what port is home. Is she allergic to penicillin? Did her grandfather have red hair? Is she part Irish? Was she conceived in love? Was she really wanted? Is there someone out there who bears her likeness?

It's been difficult for all of us. How can any of us go forward until we know what is behind us?

Love? People talk about it like it's the universal Band-Aid for all physical and emotional ailments. Well, there's one thing it can't cure. The rejection by a woman who gave her life.

We tried. The photo albums, the birthday parties, the instant set of grandparents, but in her heart she stands like a waif on the outside of a family, never feeling like she really belongs on the inside.

I look at you and I don't know why all these years I've felt threatened by the ghost of a "real mother."

You want to know what "real" is?

Real is what gets a part-time job to pay for a baton that lights up.

Real is what hears, "I hate you" and still says, "No."

Real is what sits up until 3 AM when she has the car out and it's raining.

Real is hurting when she's in pain and laughing when she's happy.

Real is emergency rooms, PTA's, music that deafens, lies, defiance, and slammed doors.

Real is what shows up every day!

I'm shouting and I don't know why.

I do know why. All these years, you have been the object of my love and gratitude, frustration and pain, blame and compassion. But mostly you have been the object of my envy. You had that wonderful experience that I would have given anything to have. The movement inside me of a girl child who would one day look at me and see me as "real."

No one can give it to me. No one can take it away from you.

It is there.

**26**

# Five Classic Motherhood Speeches

Written, choreographed, and staged for amateur
presentation
(*Advanced Mothers)

1. **"Why you cannot have a snake for a pet."**

2. **"So you've decided to pierce your ears."**

3. **"Do you know what time it is?"**

4. **"You want to borrow my <u>WHAT</u>?"**

*5. **"Don't pretend you don't know what this is all about. <u>YOU</u> know!"**

## 1. "Why you cannot have a snake for a pet."

*Scene:* Kitchen table, where a large mound of cookies sits on a plate next to a pitcher of cold milk. Mother exudes love throughout monologue.

Mother: "Sweetheart, you know that Mommy and Daddy love you very much. We would certainly never say no to your having a snake. After all, we love animals as much as you do. We just want to talk about it first.

"Have a cookie.

"Our first concern, of course, is for the snake. You know how prejudice and ignorance haunt them wherever they go. Could you stand to walk into a crowded room with your little friend and watch it empty out in three seconds? Of course not. It would break your heart.

"And they're so small. What if someone stepped on one of them with a large rake or accidentally dropped a boulder on him? It wouldn't have a chance, now would it? Sometimes, snakes have been known to give Mommy a start. Remember the one in the back yard last year that was thirty-five feet long, had fangs that dripped human blood, was pregnant, and had the capacity to open doors with a passkey?

"You may remember it as smaller, but Mommy doesn't forget things like that. Have another cookie.

"He'd be difficult to paper-train, and the poor little thing couldn't bark when he wanted to be let out or walk on a leash at the shopping center. He couldn't even chase a ball and pant.

"Sweetheart, we want a snake just as much as you do, but what kind of people would we be to deprive him of a normal life, if you get my drift. Don't you think he'd want to date and have a family and do all those things you can't do in a hermetically sealed Mason jar?

"Have all the cookies you want, dear.

"I wish serpents had a better image. You know and I know that they are just as afraid of us as we are of them. I mean just because we never saw a snake spot a human being in the grass and hyperventilate and sink into a coma doesn't mean they don't have feelings.

"Then it's settled. You tell _____ (name of playmate) it's nice of him to think of you and to want to give you his snake, but a snake needs the stability of a family unit.

"I know. It may seem like we are a stable family unit, dear, but tell him if that snake comes into this house, your mother is running away from home and never coming back!"

## 2. "So you've decided to pierce your ears."

*Scene:* Mother is seated at center stage, engaged in something domestic like reading the *American Journal of Tooth Decay* and making notes in the margins.

Daughter enters stage left.

Daughter: "What would you say if I told you I was going to pierce my ears?"

Mother (putting book down and marking spot): "My feeling is that your body is your own and if a girl wants to punch holes in her earlobes with an ice pick, it's strictly her own business. After all, darling, we don't live in a Victorian age anymore. This is _____ (current year). Every woman is a human being in her own right and it is her decision to make and if you are thinking of piercing your ears it will be over my dead body! I did not pump you full of vitamins and fix your feet to have some bungling butcher perform back-street surgery on my only daughter.

"I suppose _____ (name of daughter's best friend) is going to do it. I know she's your best friend and you'll hate me for saying this, but _____ (name of daughter's best friend) seems to have cast a spell over you. Don't misunderstand me. She's a nice girl, but I don't relish the idea of your going under the needle with a girl who plays with her gum and never washes her hands after she plays with the dog. The next thing she'll have you tattooing butterflies on your shoulder blades.

"I wasn't going to tell you about _____ (name of person she doesn't know) but she pierced her ears and suffered a concussion. She'll never be right. Had her ears 'done' in the main aisle of _____ (leading department store), passed out, and hit her head on a footstool in Better Shoes.

"You do what you want with my blessing. Why not? I'll be dead soon anyway."

## 3. "Do you know what time it is?"

*Scene:* Mother is alone on stage with television set flashing test pattern. A clock with large face is located on table next to her. She is facing the door when son or daughter walks in.

Mother: "I don't want to know where you've been, what you've been doing, or who you've been doing it with. It's late and we'll discuss it in the morning. (Turns off TV set and all the lights except one.)

"Do you honestly think that by not talking about it it's going to go away? (Son opens mouth to speak.)

"Don't lie to me! I would rather you go to bed and say nothing than to stand there and tell me you ran out of gas or the car broke down. I don't want to talk about it tonight or I'll say something I'll be sorry for. Go to bed. (Races him to landing of stairs/hallway, blocking entrance to stairs.)

"Do you have any idea what it is like to be a mother and sit here half-crazed for seven hours, hoping against hope that you were in an accident and had amnesia and that when the ambulance passed the house you heard your dog barking and it triggered your memory? I cannot believe you had the nerve to walk in here without a scratch on you and expect me to understand.

"Please, not another word. I'm exhausted. (Turns off light and follows him upstairs.)

"You know what really hurts? I've been sitting in that chair for seven hours making myself sick and you don't even have the courtesy to phone and say, 'I'm all right. Go to bed.' If you didn't want to talk to me, you could have paid someone to do it for you. Go ahead, say it. You didn't ask me to wait up. I wondered when you'd get around to that. I'm supposed to have a little switch that clicks on and off? On, when it's fun to be a mother. Off, when it's five o'clock in the morning? (Bathroom door slams and she stands outside it.)

"Well, I don't know about you, but I'm going to bed. The doctor says I need at least eight hours of sleep a night. Easy for him to say. He's never had an ungrateful son. Never sat there for seven hours trying to figure out what two people could possibly do at five in the morning. (Bathroom door opens and son goes to bedroom door and closes it.)

"I know you want me to hear your story—if you have one. I personally think we'll be a little more rational in the morning. If you want to apologize, I could heat up the chili."

## 4. "You want to borrow my WHAT?"

*Scene:* Mother is busy while child hovers nearby, uncertain. Mother has a distinct advantage and is in charge of this situation.

Mother: "I know that look. You're standing there because you want to borrow something. If it's my hair dryer, you've already got it, unless it grew legs and walked back into my bathroom. I'm not a selfish person. You know that. I don't mind if you borrow something as long as you return it in the same condition as I loaned it to you.

"Take my luggage. Which you did, literally. What did you carry in it? Scrap iron? The whole frame is bent. And my camera will never be the same since you dropped it in the sand. Every picture we develop comes out looking like a puzzle.

"Remember my tennis racket you borrowed three years ago? You never did replace the string you broke. Lucky it's the one in the middle and I never hit the ball there.

(Refrain: I'm-not-a-selfish-person speech.)

"I wouldn't mind lending you things if you took care of them. I guess I don't have to remind you of my good white blouse that you promised not to sweat in and did. The only place I can wear it now is to funerals where I don't have to raise my arms.

"The trouble with kids is they don't know the value of what they're borrowing and don't have respect for it.

"Do you remember how you returned my car the last time you borrowed it? It had trash all over the back, mud on the tires, catsup on the steering wheel, and I don't have proof, but I know the clutch had been violated.

"You want to borrow my WHAT? Sit down! Let me tell you why I'm going to say no."

ERMA BOMBECK

## *5. "Don't pretend you don't know what this is all about. <u>YOU</u> know!"

*Scene:* Anywhere. Mother's face is a mask that reveals nothing and reacts to nothing that is said. *This is important*, lest the child know what you are talking about. Keep clues broad. Interest is sustained by slamming doors, dropping plates on the table, and kicking the dog.

Mother: "Well, I hope you're satisfied. You've done it again. Don't pretend you don't know what this is all about. *You* know. How long before you were going to tell me about it?

"Did it ever occur to you to check with me first? That's it, play dumb. You're dumb like a fox. You knew what this would do to your _____ (person, place, or thing). You've done it before.

"I'd like to say it doesn't matter, but it does. Well, no use crying over spilled milk.

"And don't play Miss (Mr.) Innocence with me. You know very well what I'm talking about. It's not the first time you've disappointed me and I'm sure it won't be the last. If you want to talk about it, I'm here to listen. If you don't, tough biscuits.

"I'd like to think you'd promise not to do it again, but I know you won't, so forget it. You want a hint as to what I'm talking about? That's a joke. Do you mean to stand there and tell me you haven't the foggiest notion of why I'm angry? That's rich. Really rich.

"Okay, I'll play your little game. Tuesday! Is that enough of a hint? You know you should be an actress (actor). I am looking at an Academy Award performance here. You

*Speech for Advanced Mothers with years of experience.

can make your eyes as big as a spare tire, but you won't convince me you don't know what I'm talking about.

"I'm going to say this once and only once. If you ever do it again, you're going to have to answer to a lot more people than me.

"You have anything to say? Any apologies to make? Any promises?

"You know something? I'll never understand you."

**27**

*What kind of a mother would . . .*
**rather be rich and thin than pregnant?**

# Sarah

There are three things in this world that people refuse to accept: an incurable bad back, directions without a map, and a woman who does not want a child.

Sarah did not want a child. She was thirty-two, happy with her marriage, happy with her job, and happy with her life. What she was unhappy about was the people around her who seemed to feel her choice not to have children was their business.

People like her mother, her sister Gracie (mother of five), her best friend Dodie, and her gynecologist, who reminded her, "You're not getting any younger." (Who is?)

One day, in a moment of intimacy when she and her mother were alone, Sarah attempted one last time to explain to her mother why she preferred to remain childless.

"Try to understand, Mom," she said. "I'm not against children. I'm just against them for me. For Gracie, it's fine. She's a born mother. I just don't want to go through life with little gates all over the house and a bathtub full of ducks and boats. People who have children change, and it's scary. They lose a part of themselves that I don't want to lose. It's like someone flipping a switch. All of a sudden you're not a person anymore. You're attached to another human being. Separate them and they both die.

"I don't want to be an extension of someone else's fever, someone else's hunger, pain, disappointment, and frustration. I had a wonderful childhood, but when I was a child I never began to appreciate all your work and sacrifice. What did you get out of it? A lot of slammed doors and a wooden pig that held recipes for your birthday.

"If I had children, Mom, I'd be having them for all the wrong reasons—because you wanted to be a grandmother or Steve wanted someone to carry on his name or I couldn't stand the pressure of people wanting to know why I don't have children.

"I don't think I'm selfish. I'm certainly not bitter or angry. I just feel I have a choice and I have every right to make it. Do you understand?"

Her mother nodded.

The next morning, in a planned moment of intimacy, Sarah's mother called her other daughter, Gracie, and said, "I think I know why your sister doesn't want a child."

Gracie glued the receiver to her ear. "Why?"

"Well," said her mother, "I don't pretend to understand all of what she said, so I'll quote verbatim. She's scared! It's that simple. The idea of having a baby scares her spitless, and besides, she doesn't want all the mess around the house, like rubber boats and gates.

"She made it pretty clear that if I want to be a grandmother again, it's in your ballpark, since you love the crud detail. Besides, she said with her luck she'd catch a fever from them and probably eat every time they ate and weigh a ton. Does that make sense to you?"

"Perfectly," said Gracie.

Within the hour, Gracie called Dodie, Sarah's best friend, and said, "Hold on to your hat. You know how none of us could figure why Sarah shouldn't have a child and be as miserable as the rest of us? Well, Mom talked with her this morning and she finally confessed."

"What's her problem?" asked Dodie.

"I couldn't believe it when Mom told me. Sarah is afraid of losing her shape! She never weighed over 115 pounds in her entire life."

"I think I've heard about that," said Dodie. "It's called sagophobia. It's a fear of the entire body falling down around your knees."

"And listen to this," interrupted Gracie, "she said that if anyone in the family should have a packful of kids, it's me. How do you like that? She said I've always got a houseful of old gates and soldiers and boats all over the place, but I'm used to it.

"She didn't say it in so many words, but Mom guessed the real reason is that Sarah is up for promotion and she can't afford to pass it up. I'm not too shocked, are you?"

"Not really," said Dodie.

When her husband came home, Dodie handed him a drink and said, "You'll never guess what Sarah's sister told me today."

"Surprise me," said Bob, opening up the paper and burying himself behind it.

"She said Sarah wants a baby, but they can't afford one. And all this time she's been putting up such a brave front and all, pretending she didn't want one. Gracie said she's up for promotion if she can keep her weight under 115. I don't know what they're going to do if she doesn't get it. Obviously Steve's job is on shaky ground. They won't even be able to adopt. I wonder why they bought a boat? Are you listening to me?"

"I heard every word," said Bob.

Several days later, while playing handball with Sarah's father, Bob said, "Congratulations. I hear Steve and Sarah are adopting a Korean child and going boating this summer if he can turn his career around."

That night, Sarah's father said to her mother, "Have you talked to Sarah lately?"

"Not in the last day or two."

"I heard the strangest rumor at the gym today. Something about Sarah wanting to adopt, but Steve doesn't want to. Does that make sense to you?"

"Perfectly," said his wife.

Exactly one week from the time they had their "little talk," Sarah's mother paid her daughter a visit, looked her in the eyes, kissed her on the cheek, and said, "I want you to know that whatever your decision for your future, your father and I will support you a hundred percent. I know now why you said the things you did and we love you for it."

As Sarah told Steve that night, "Imagine my thinking my mother wouldn't understand a word of what I was saying. Sometimes I think we underrate mothers."

**28**

# Motherese

It's a language unto its own, spoken and passed down from one mother to another.

There are hundreds of phrases. The following ones will get a mother through the first seventeen years of a child's life.

## Oldies But Goodies

THIS IS GOING TO HURT ME WORSE THAN IT HURTS YOU.

WHEN YOU GROW UP, YOU'LL THANK ME FOR BEING SO STRICT.

WE'LL SEE.

DON'T TALK WITH FOOD IN YOUR MOUTH. ANSWER ME!

I'M DOING THIS BECAUSE I LOVE YOU.

NEVER MIND, I'LL DO IT MYSELF.

I'M NOT GOING TO SPEAK TO YOU AGAIN.

LITTLE PITCHERS HAVE BIG EARS.

CHILDREN SHOULD BE SEEN AND NOT HEARD.
NO SENSE CRYING OVER SPILT MILK.
DO YOU BELIEVE EVERYTHING YOU HEAR?
I'LL GIVE YOU SOMETHING TO CRY ABOUT.
KEEP YOUR HANDS WHERE THEY'RE SUPPOSED
TO BE.

## On Age

WHY DON'T YOU GROW UP?

SOMEDAY YOU'LL BE OLD.

YOU'RE NOT GETTING ANY YOUNGER.

YOU'LL GROW UP FAST ENOUGH. WHEN I WAS
YOUR AGE . . .

WHEN ARE YOU GOING TO ACT YOUR AGE?

I'LL TREAT YOU LIKE AN ADULT WHEN YOU
START ACTING LIKE ONE.

YOU'LL ALWAYS BE MAMA'S BABY.

## Guilt Grabbers

I'M GOING TO SEND ALL THAT FOOD YOU LEFT
ON YOUR PLATE TO ALL THE STARVING
ARMENIANS.

DO YOU WANT MOMMY TO LEAVE THE HOUSE
AND NEVER COME BACK?

IF YOU SLEEP WITH DOGS, YOU GET FLEAS.

YOU'RE GOING TO DRIVE ME TO AN EARLY
GRAVE.

BE GLAD I'M SCREAMING. WHEN I STOP . . .

THIS IS THE LAST TIME I'M GOING TO BEG.

WE'RE NOT ASKING YOU NOT TO GET MARRIED.
WE'RE JUST ASKING YOU TO WAIT.

JUST KEEP PLAYING WITH MATCHES AND YOU'LL
WET THE BED.

THAT'S WHAT YOU GET FOR NOT LISTENING.

I'M ONLY ONE PERSON.

## Great Exit Lines

JUST WAIT TILL YOU HAVE CHILDREN OF YOUR
OWN!

DO YOU THINK I WAS BORN YESTERDAY?

IF YOU DON'T LISTEN, YOU'RE GOING TO HAVE
TO FEEL.

THAT DOES IT. I'M SENDING YOU TO REFORM
SCHOOL.

WHERE DID I FAIL?

WHY ME, GOD?

## Philosophical Bon-Bons

YOU MADE YOUR BED, NOW LIE IN IT.

I MAY NOT ALWAYS UNDERSTAND YOU, BUT I
AM ALWAYS WILLING TO LISTEN.

WHAT'S A MOTHER FOR BUT TO SUFFER?

FOOL ME ONCE, SHAME ON ME—FOOL ME TWICE,
I'LL KILL YOU.

IF YOUR GIRLFRIEND JUMPED OFF THE BRIDGE
WOULD YOU DO IT TOO?

IF YOU FALL OFF THAT SWING AND BREAK A
LEG, DON'T COME RUNNING TO ME.

**29**

*What kind of a mother would...*
**have Joan Crawford for a role model?**

# Janet

It was a masculine house. You could tell just by looking at the outside of it that inside all the toilet seats were up.

The yard looked like a missile site. The front door was held open by flyers and throwaways. Someone had drawn a sixth finger on the HELPING HAND sign in the window and added, ALL MAJOR CREDIT CARDS ACCEPTED.

The driveway looked like a used car lot. Janet's compact brought the total number to six. As she balanced four bags of groceries, she kicked open the door with her foot. The dog nearly knocked her over trying to get out.

God, wouldn't you think they'd get a clue that the dog wanted out when he tunneled under the door? Janet's eyes took in the kitchen.

Breakfast cereal had hardened in the bowl. The butter had turned into a beverage. The kitchen phone was off the hook. The TV was blaring. Mechanically, she put the milk in the refrigerator before moving down the hall. At a bedroom door she yelled, "Mark! Turn that stereo down or put on your headphones."

When he didn't answer, her suspicions were confirmed. The music fed into his ears and blared out of his nose. The next stop was her bathroom, where she pushed in the lock button and caught a glimpse of herself in the mirror. She wasn't your basic Oil of Olay success story. At forty-six, Janet's hair was coming in Brillo gray and zinging out in every direction. Every muscle in her body had surrendered to gravity. (She dropped out of aerobics class when the only thing she could touch were her knees to her chest . . . and only because her chest met her knees halfway.)

This had been the worst day of her life! Her best friend was happy because she was going on a cruise. The elastic broke on her maternity underwear (she wasn't pregnant), and her dentist had just informed her her gums were receding. Someday she'd put her body together.

All her friends had, but then all her friends didn't have three full-grown sons at home squatting in the nest with knife and fork poised, waiting for her to come home from work each night and drop something from the microwave into their beaks.

The children of her contemporaries were long gone. They were living with someone, bumming around with guitars on their backs, having babies, or wrestling with high interest rates.

At first, she was flattered that her kids never wanted Mother's Day to end. That was before Joan Crawford became her role model. Now, she just felt used.

The porch light had been burning day and night for three years.

The refrigerator held empty milk cartons, dried out lunch meat, and empty ice cube trays.

They borrowed her hair dryer, camera, luggage, car, and money without asking.

They kept hours like hamsters.

They were still small, dependent children in big hairy bodies with deep voices.

What was she supposed to do? Turn her back on them when they needed her? Was it John's fault his marriage hadn't worked out? Cindy had seemed so perfect for him. They had everything in common. Both loved raw pizza dough, both were left-handed, and both liked the way Liza Minnelli sang "New York, New York" better than Frank Sinatra.

It should have worked.

Then there was Peter. At twenty-four (two years younger than John) he was well on his way to becoming the oldest living schoolboy in North America. He had changed his major twelve times, having passed only two things last semester: human sexuality and his eye test.

As for Mark, Janet was convinced his future was shaped when, in her eighth month, she got caught in a revolving door. It was to have a serious effect on her youngest. His first words were "hello-goodbye."

Their relationship had never been good. She honestly never knew why. When anyone asked her how many children she had, she'd say, "Four. John, Peter, Mark at home, and Mark away from home."

Mark at home was miserable. He was the most negative kid Janet had ever set eyes on. There was no pleasing him. No one ever cooked his favorite food. Everyone picked on him. He hated his room. He hated his clothes. He hated his life.

For the last three years, he'd worked on and off, but mostly he sat in his room strumming his guitar and waiting for a dish to rattle.

Janet slipped into her robe and gave a last glance in the mirror. Would there ever be a day when she and George would pick at a salad by candlelight and hoist a glass of white wine without him saying, "My God! Smell this. This glass was used for creme rinse."

As she turned to run water for a quick shower she saw it. Her bottle of Gossamer Gold shampoo that contained pure organic honey herbs and H-D phylferrous additive that was to make her a legend in her own time was on its side with the cap off. All $4.69 of it had gone down the drain. She had hidden it carefully behind the Ace bandages and a box of Midol and "they" had found it.

That shampoo was more than her ticket to *fat*, sexy hair. It was her last bastion of privacy, her only selfish indulgence that separated her from all that *gusto!*

She had had it with their insensitivity, their noisy mouths that every night at the dinner table attacked food like scissors, their mildewed towels, their tennis balls under the brake pedal.

She was sick of hearing a siren in the middle of the night and not being able to go back to sleep until all the cars were in. She was exhausted from sharing their lives and their problems. As a mother, she had stayed too long at the fair.

Outraged, she stomped out of the bathroom and beat with both fists on Mark's door. When no one answered, she barged in. He was propped up in bed, bare-chested with his headphones on, strumming his guitar.

"Did you wash your hair today?" she demanded.

He shook his head.

"You're lying. I know fat, sensuous hair when I see it."

"Okay, so I borrowed some shampoo. I'll pay you back."

"The Martins are going on a cruise. My elastic broke,

my gums are shrinking and you're going to pay me back."

"What are your gums shrinking from?"

"My teeth!"

"I suppose you're gonna rehash how much my teeth cost and how ticked off you were when I dated the girl with the overbite."

"I was ticked off because the woman was thirty-three years old and it was her eleven-year-old daughter who had the overbite."

She looked around the room. Like its occupant, it was half child, half man. The wrestling trophy from his junior year in high school was on the nightstand along with a suspicious letter that said FINAL NOTICE and had a return address of Municipal Court, Division of Traffic. Clothes dotted the floor, newspapers were draped from chairs, and a sherbet glass with something brown in it was under the bed. "This room is a dump!" she said. "How can you breathe in here? It's June, for God's sake, what's your ski sweater doing out?"

Mark looked at her closely. "Why don't you get it over with? Tell us all to leave."

"What are you talking about?"

"Boot us out. Clean house."

"Don't think it hasn't crossed my mind." She looked desperately for a place to sit down. "I've tried to be a good mother, Mark. And a patient one. I really have."

"You've been a good mother," he said evenly. "So finish your job."

"What do you mean finish my job?"

"You chickened out. All our lives you told us what to do, how to do it, and when. You've done it. You don't have to prove anything anymore. It's graduation day. Say good-bye to us and get on with your life."

"You have no right to say that to me. I've been through it all with you kids—from exhaustion to anger to guilt and back again."

"You're at martyrdom and you've been there a long time. How long can you keep bucking for Mother of the Year?"

"Is that what you think? Then why don't you move out?"

They sat there for a long time.

Finally Janet said, "What will you do? Get a job? Get married?"

"You always said there was no one good enough for me."

"That was before I knew you showered in your underwear." She smiled.

They looked at one another for a long time.

"Mom," said Mark, "I'm scared."

"Me too," said Janet, closing the door.

Her hands were shaking and she felt like she was going to cry. What if fat, sexy hair and independence were overrated? She squared her shoulders, "What the heck. Joan Crawford made it in 'Mildred Pierce.' "

**30**

# If You Can't Stand the Heat... Turn Off the Stove

In a Sunday school class one morning, the teacher asked, "And what did the disciples say before they ate the fish?"

A five-year-old boy in the front row waved his hand vigorously and said, "I know. They said, 'These fish got any bones in them?' "

As a mother who has dedicated her life to force-feeding her children, I have every reason to believe this story is gospel.

Kids are without a doubt the most suspicious diners in the world. They will eat mud (raw or baked) rocks, paste, crayons, ballpoint pens, moving goldfish, cigarette butts, and cat food.

Try to coax a little beef stew into their mouths and they look at you like a puppy when you stand over him with the Sunday paper rolled up.

I got so much food spit back in my face when my kids were small, I put windshield wipers on my glasses.

I read a survey once that said fifty-eight percent of the children interviewed resented the fact that parents make them eat food they don't like.

My children always had an unusual diet. They tolerated hot dogs only when they cost $1.50 in the ballpark, hamburgers that were 1/15 inch thick and suffocated in secret sauce, charred marshmallows that were speared on a bent coat hanger, and anything left under a car seat longer than fifteen days.

In general, they refused to eat anything that hadn't danced on TV.

By mid-1970's, I faced up to a cold, hard fact. Home cooking was dead! A victim of nutrition and a well-balanced diet served up by a mother.

Show biz food was in! Hamburgers with cute names, catchy songs about tacos, and free balloons with every shake. I did what any red-blooded American mother would do. I fought back.

I installed golden arches above the stove with an electric scoreboard and focused a red light on the pie to keep it warm.

I added a lighted menu and a drive-in window and served everything in a bag that leaked coleslaw and contained a two-inch plastic fork.

I served pizza wearing a straw hat and a cane. And when their attention began to lag, I propped my mouth open with a fork and let them yell their order into it, but it didn't work.

There's just something exciting to a child about eating in a car that smells like onions every day of the year.

For the next several years, we ate all of our meals in the car.

Then one day, our son said a curious thing. He said, "Didn't you tell me I could eat anywhere I wanted for my birthday?" We both nodded. "Then I want to eat at home."

"Well, I don't know," I said, looking at my husband. "Can we afford it?"

"Sure, what the heck, it's his birthday."

On the night of the birthday dinner, everyone even looked different. They were taller.

"Hey, look at this," said one of the boys. "What do you call these?"

"Silverware," I said. "That particular piece is a knife."

"Neat."

"And these are plates."

"I've never eaten in a place where you can take your dog before," said our daughter.

As the family sang "Happy Birthday," our son said, "Could we do this again next year? Maybe sooner?"

As I tossed the china noisily into a trash barrel, I said, "Let's not get carried away. We'll see."

# 🌸 31

# "Every Puppy Should Have a Boy"

The ad in the paper said the puppy was "partially housebroken."

That is like being "partially pregnant."

Sylvia should have known better, but she was one of thousands of mothers every year who give in to family pressure and get a dog.

The first thing Sylvia did was to set up house rules. Anyone who saw the little puddles or dog bombs first was to clean it up. Then, you were to rub his nose in it and put him outside. No one was to feed him at the table. He was to sleep only in his own bed in the utility room. Everyone would take turns putting him out and bringing him in. Praise him when he did good, punish him when he did bad.

The first week, Bob's feet never touched the floor. He was the darling of the Forbes household.

The second week, they were less enthusiastic about his being there. (One of the kids even told him to "shut up!" when he yapped in the middle of the night.)

By the third week, Bob was Sylvia's dog. She fed him, bathed him, and let him in and out fifty times a day.

One night four years later, Sylvia heard her sons whispering. One was saying, "You better clean up Bob's mess." His brother answered, "It's my year not to see it. You didn't see it last year."

She gathered the family together and said, "I thought all of you should know that we are going to be in the *Guinness Book of World Records*. Our living room carpet is now one large, continuous wall-to-wall stain. The bottom line is, I am getting a new carpet and Bob goes. Please, I don't want anyone to say anything until I am finished. Try to see Bob as I see him—a twenty-eight-year-old man in a shaggy fur coat who watches television for six hours every evening and never leaves the room for a commercial, if you get my drift.

"He knows nothing of nature. He has never seen a tree, a blade of grass, a curb, a low chair leg, or a car tire.

"He has no curiosity as to why the velvet on the chair is so hard for him to reach or why they make a shag carpet so difficult to balance yourself on on three legs.

"I have tried everything, including sawing a hole in a $300 door that lets out the heat in the winter and the cool air in the summer. Bob is out!"

Even though Sylvia went on to be elected to the U.S. Senate, write three books, and give the commencement address at Harvard, she will always be remembered as the selfish mother who put carpet before compassion.

**32**

*What kind of a mother would...*
## deny having grandchildren three times before the rooster crows?

# Treva

Treva hadn't spoken a word since they left the baby shower. As her daughter Gloria struggled to find a comfortable spot for her stomach under the steering wheel, Treva knotted her nose tissue into a ball, lost in her own thoughts.

They centered on Gloria's mother-in-law, Gayle. That woman had been bad news ever since her son married Gloria two years ago. Even at the wedding she was a royal pain. A bridegroom's mother is supposed to wear beige and keep her mouth shut. Everyone knows that. But not Gayle. She whipped around the reception like Mrs. Astor's pet horse, leaving Treva in the kitchen to slice ham like a field hand.

And the gift of a honeymoon to Acapulco made their bathroom heater look sick!

To make matters worse, Gloria thought the sun rose and set in the woman's backyard. Now she was trying to take over on the baby her daughter was carrying—Treva's first grandchild!

"You're quiet, Mom," said Gloria. "Did you have a

good time? Can you believe how many prizes Gayle won? Imagine getting twenty-three words out of the word BAS-SINET. You never said how many you got."

"One," said Treva—"ASS!"

"Mother!" she said. "Shame on you." Then, following a silence, "Did you hear that Gayle is going to videotape the birth of our baby?"

"Pull the car over. I'm going to throw up," said Treva.

"Mom," said Gloria softly, "there's no reason for you to be jealous of Gayle. It's your grandchild too and both of you will get equal time with it."

"Jealous! Is that what you think I am?" Treva laughed in a high-pitched voice. "Don't be ridiculous. The baby won't be able to tell us apart, except I'll be the grandmother who bought him a stuffed teddy bear and Gayle will be the grandmother who bought him the San Diego Zoo. Let's drop it. How do you feel about ham?"

"Compared to what?" asked Gloria.

"I'm trying to figure out what to have for Christmas dinner."

"Mom! It's five months away. We haven't had Thanksgiving yet."

"Thanksgiving is settled. We're having your favorite, turkey."

Gloria slowed down and lowered her voice. "Mom, we've been through all of this before. Chuck and I just can't go on every holiday hopping from one house to another eating for four people—five this year. I'm going to weigh 500 pounds trying to keep all of the parents happy."

"Look, if you want to go to Gayle's, just say so. I've lived with disappointment before, I can do it again."

Gloria stopped the car and turned toward her mother.

"Mom, do you remember the old story about the wise king and the two women fighting over a child?"

Treva shook her head stubbornly.

"Each woman claimed the child was hers. Finally, the wise old king put the baby on a table before him, picked up a sword and said, 'Very well, since neither of you can decide, I will cut the baby in half.' At that moment, in an unselfish act of love, the real mother rushed forward and said, 'No! Give the baby to her.' At that moment, the king knew who the real mother was. Do you understand what that story is saying, Mother?"

Treva looked at her daughter with tears in her eyes. "It is saying Gayle kept her mouth shut and gets custody of the new grandchild and I get stuck with a twenty-pound turkey and a ten-pound ham!"

That night in bed Treva couldn't sleep. She kept seeing Gayle, who began to look like Rosalind Russell as Auntie Mame, waving from a cruise ship with her grandchild by her side and throwing streamers and promising to write.

She hated herself for being so competitive, but her arms ached to hold a baby once more. She had never adjusted to the empty nest. Maybe if she set up a nursery in the spare room, Gloria would leave the baby here on weekends. New parents always need time to themselves. Perhaps she and Mel could even take their grandchild to Florida with them and build sand castles on the beach.

She fell asleep fantasizing about a tall dark stranger saying, "You don't look old enough to be a mother," only to have her blush and say, "I'm not. It's my grandchild!"

## TREVA . . . TEN YEARS LATER

The minute they heard Gloria's car in the driveway, Treva and her husband swung into action with all the precision and efficiency of the Lippizan cavalry.

Treva whipped the planter off the coffee table and put it in the hall closet, locked the bathroom door, shoved a bowl of candy under the lounge chair, put the dog in the utility room, and took the knob off the TV set and dropped it in her pocket.

Her husband Mel covered the sofa with plastic, put his bowling trophy on top of the refrigerator, blocked the entrance to the basement with a kitchen chair, put the toaster cover over the phone, and closed the lid on the piano to cover the keys.

Then both put toothpicks in their mouths to announce they had just eaten.

They broke their own record—one minute, thirty-six seconds.

Gloria dragged in with her four children under eight years of age and fell into a chair. The children scattered as though they ran on batteries, except Jeffrey, who sat in the middle of the floor and screamed.

"What's the matter with him?" asked Treva.

"He's teething," said Gloria tiredly.

"Have you tried a little whiskey on the gums?" asked Treva.

"I had a belt just before I came and I feel better," said Gloria.

"So what brings you to the neighborhood?"

"Nothing in particular. You got any crackers?" she asked, going to the kitchen and flinging open the doors. "Would you look at this. Wild rice! There was never any wild rice when I lived at home."

"You hate rice."

"I might have developed a taste for it if I knew it cost this much. So what time are you having Thanksgiving dinner?"

Treva and Mel exchanged glances.

"Ah, we're not going to be home this year for Thanksgiving, dear," Treva said quickly. "We're going out. Mel, check on Danny, the toilet's running."

"Do you know how long it's been since we've spent a holiday together?"

"What about Gayle?" asked Treva. "Gloria! Where is Jeffrey's diaper?"

"He just started taking it off when it has a load in it. Go get your diaper, Jeffrey. I know . . . poopoo. Gayle? They're going on a holiday cruise again. If I didn't know better, I'd feel no one wanted us for the holidays."

"Sweetheart, you don't want to chew on that cassette. Give it to Grandma. And don't cry!"

"Mother, when you take away something, you have to give her something else."

"I'm about to," said Treva, raising her hand.

"It's a shame you don't have that roomful of toys like you used to. That kept 'em busy. Do you really use that room for a chapel?"

"There isn't a day I don't go in there and meditate," said Treva. "What about Gayle? Does she still have her nursery-away-from-home?"

"No, she converted it to a tack room three years ago."

"A tack room in the house?"

"Doesn't matter. They don't have horses anyway. Well, listen, I've got to get going. You'll call on Thanksgiving?"

"Of course I will. Melanie! That's Grandma's dusting powder and it cost $12.50 a box. You must leave it here. You can visit it the next time you come. Melanie, don't take that lid off! Please!"

"You want me to clean it up?" said Gloria.

"No, I can do it when you leave," said Treva. "Take care of yourself, dear, and . . . don't turn your back on them."

**138**

As the car pulled out of the driveway, Treva and Mel mechanically and without words went about a ritual they had done many times before.

Treva put a sponge in each hand and began moving quickly through the rooms sliding her hands up and down the door frames, the refrigerator, and the cabinets. She let the dog out of the utility room, put the knobs back on the TV set, and brought the planter back into the daylight.

Mel wheeled out the sweeper and vacuumed up crumbs and dusting powder. He retrieved his bowling trophy from the refrigerator and turned off the spigots in the bathtub. The candy went back on the table.

As Treva picked three Band-Aids off the wall in the foyer, Mel rubbed out a white spot on the piano bench where a wet glass had been.

As Treva headed for the chapel, Mel said, "Remember that first Thanksgiving when Gloria didn't come home and you draped her chair in black bunting and put her picture in the empty chair?"

Treva winced. "Give it a rest, Mel."

**33**

*I cannot possibly improve or add anything to this anonymous letter received in May, 1982, from a mother in upstate New York.*
*She belongs in this book.*

# Anonymous

Dear Erma:

You feel like my best friend. The only thing that surprised me was to find out that I am taller than you.

Anyway, I have something I want to talk to you about. There is no solution to this. I just want to let you know we exist, we are human too and we hurt with the helplessness I can't begin to describe.

I belong to a group of people that doesn't even know it's a group. We have no organization, no meetings, no spokespersons, we don't even know each other. Each of us, as individuals, are way in the back of the closet with the rats and cockroaches. We may not even be any different from our neighbors. We look the same, talk and act the same, yet when people know our secret, they shun us as lepers.

We are the parents of criminals. We too love our children. We too tried to bring them up the best way we knew how. There is small solace in reading of a movie star or politician's kid being arrested. It helps but little to realize that our pain is not confined to the poor. (Although studies have shown that a rich kid is more likely to be sent home with a reprimand from the police, where a poor kid will wind up in jail.)

We are the visitors. Mother's Day, Christmas, our kids cannot come to us, so we go to them. For some of us, the hurt is so unbearable, we cut out the cause—we give up on them. Some parents don't visit, don't write, don't acknowledge the living human being they bore.

I have not yet given up on my son, though the court has. I still cry, and plead, and encourage and pray. And I still love him.

I search my memory. Where did I fail him? My son was planned, wanted, and was exactly the all-around kid I had hoped for. I spent lots of time with him, reading stories, going for walks, playing catch, teaching him to fly a kite. We went to church together every Sunday since he was 4. He did all right in school and his teachers liked him. He had lots of friends, and they were always playing ball or going fishing, all the regular kid things. He was on Little League. I went to every game. He won a trophy for All-Stars. He was just a regular kid.

That's only one. Mine. There are thousands of them. Criminals with ordinary childhoods. We, their parents, trying to live ordinary lives. And maybe being ostracized by family members and certainly by society. ("Maybe it's contagious!")

Tomorrow is Mother's Day. My son is running from the police. I didn't do it, I don't condone it, nor try to justify what he did. But I still love him, and it hurts.

I hope you can find room in your heart to accept us, who love the children society hates.

I'm sure you understand why I just cannot put my name. Thanks for letting me get it off my chest.

"Mom"

And I know you know that this is not a made-up letter. I'm real. I wish I weren't. Happy Mother's Day.

**34**

# "Don't You Dare Bleed on Mom's Breakfast"

A lot of things have been done in bed in the name of love . . . but nothing comes close to the traditional Mother's Day breakfast in bed.

On this day, all over the country, mothers are pushed back into their pillows, their bird of paradise (which blooms every other year for fifteen minutes) is snipped and put in a shot glass, and a strange assortment of food comes out of a kitchen destined to take the sight out of a good eye.

A mixer whirs out of control, then stops abruptly as a voice cries, "I'm telling."

A dog barks and another voice says, "Get his paws out of there. Mom has to eat that!"

Minutes pass and finally, "Dad! Where's the chili sauce?"

Then, "Don't you dare bleed on Mom's breakfast."

The rest is a blur of banging doors, running water, rapid footsteps and finally, "You started the fire; *you* put it out!"

The breakfast is fairly standard: A water tumbler of juice, five pieces of black bacon that snap in half when you breathe on them, a mound of eggs that would feed a Marine division, and four pieces of cold toast. They line up on the bed to watch you eat and from time to time ask why you're not drinking your Kool-Aid or touching the cantaloupe with black olives on top spelling out M-O-M.

Later that night, after you have decided it's easier to move to a new house than clean the kitchen, you return to your bed, where you encounter beneath the blanket either (a) a black jelly bean, (b) a plantar's wart, or (c) a black olive that put the O in M-O-M.

And if you're wise, you'll reflect on this day. For the first time, your children gave instead of received. They offered up to you the sincerest form of flattery—trying to emulate what you would do for them. They gave you one of the greatest gifts people can give: themselves.

There will be other Mother's Days and a parade of gifts that will astound and amaze you, but not one of them will ever measure up to the sound of your children in the kitchen on Mother's Day whispering, "Don't you dare bleed on Mom's breakfast."

**35**

# "Is Anyone Home?"

In 1981, Miriam Volhouse was the only full-time, stay-at-home mother in her block. She was also named in the school records of seventeen kids who listed her under IN CASE OF EMERGENCY CALL . . .

Occasionally Miriam was tempted to join her friends in an outside job, but she resisted because she considered herself a conscientious mother and "rapping" with one's children was important.

Each evening when Miriam heard a door slam, she'd yell, "Mark, is that you?"

"What do you want? Buzz is waiting. We're going to shoot baskets."

"Can't we just sit and have a conversation?"

"I gotta go," he'd say.

Miriam would pour two glasses of milk and put cookies on a plate and grope her way through the dark living room. "You in here, Ben?"

"Shhhhh."

"So, what kind of a day did you have? I'll bet there are a lot of fun things you'd like to share. I tried a new recipe today and . . ."

"Mom! Give me a break. I'm watching 'M*A*S*H!' "

When another door slammed, Miriam would race feverishly in time to see Wendy writing a note, "Don't wait dinner. Choir practice."

"Wendy, I want you to know I'm here if you want to rap about anything . . . like I want to know how you feel about life."

"I'm for it," she said, pulling on her coat, and then added, "Mom, you've got to get something to do. You can't lean on your kids all the time for companionship."

As Miriam drank both glasses of milk and ate the plateful of cookies, she felt rejected. No one was ever home when she was. Kids shouldn't have parents, if that's how they're going to treat them. What if something happened to her? Who would know? They were selfish and thought only of themselves. She couldn't remember the last time they sat down and talked with her about her problems or her day. How did other mothers get their children to talk to them?

She found out. Miriam got a job.

Every day between 3 and 6 PM Miriam felt like an 800 number for free records. Her kids were on the phone to her every three minutes, each time with a new trauma. She couldn't get them to stop talking. In desperation, Miriam posted a list of rules regarding phone calls.

**1.** If there is an emergency, ask yourself, "Will Mom drop dead when she hears this? Can she find a plumber after six? Will she carry out her threat to move to another city and change her name?"

**2.** If there is blood to report, consider these questions: Is it yours? Your brother's? Is there a lot? A little? On the sofa that is not Scotchgarded?

**3.** When every kid in the neighborhood decides the house would be a neat place to play because there's no adult at home, ask yourself, "Do I want to spend my entire puberty locked in my room with no food and no television? Do I need the friendship of a boy who throws ice cubes at birds? Will Mom notice we made confetti in her blender?"

**4.** Only a fool calls his mother and says, "There's nothing to do."

One night, as she was racing through the kitchen and running the hamburger through the dry cycle to thaw and delegating chores to the kids, her son said, "If you're not going to stay home and take care of us, how come you had children?"

Her other son said, "There's no one here anymore when I come home from school. You used to bake cookies."

Her daughter said, "Sometimes I think mothers are selfish. They don't share any of their innermost thoughts with you, like how they feel about life . . ."

"I'm for it," said Miriam, tossing the salad.

**36**

# Primer of Guilt
# "Bless Me, Everybody, for
# I Have Sinned"

**A** Abandoning children and responsibility, leaving them helpless and alone with a $200 babysitter, a $3,700 entertainment center, a freezer full of food, and $600 worth of toys while you and your husband have a fun time attending a funeral in Ames, Iowa.

**B** Buying a store-bought cake for your son's first birthday.

**C** Cursing your only daughter with your kinky red hair and your only son with your shortness.

**D** Dumping cheap shampoo into a bottle of the children's Natural Herbal Experience, which costs $5 a throw.

**E** Explaining to "baby" of family why the only thing in his baby book are his footprint, a poem by Rod McKuen, and a recipe for carrot cake.

*f* Flushing a lizard down the toilet and telling child it got a phone call saying there was trouble at home.

*G* Going home from the hospital after hysterectomy and apologizing to kids for not bringing them anything.

*h* Hiding out in the bathroom when the kids are calling for you all over the house.

*I* Indulging yourself by napping and when caught with chenille marks on your face telling your children it's a rash.

*J* Jamming down the sewer three newspapers you promised your child with a broken arm you'd deliver for him.

*k* Keeping Godiva chocolates in TEA canister and telling yourself kids don't appreciate good chocolate.

*L* Laundering daughter's $40 wool sweater in hot water.

*M* Missing a day calling Mother.

*N* Never loaning your car to anyone you've given birth to.

*O* Overreacting to child who found your old report card stuck in a book by threatening to send him to a box number in Hutchinson, Kansas, if he talks.

*P* Pushing grocery cart out of store and forgetting baby in another cart inside until you have turned on the ignition.

**Q** Quarreling with son about homework only to do it for him and getting a C on it.

**R** Refusing to bail out daughter who lives by credit cards alone.

**S** Sewing a mouse on the shirt pocket of son who is far-sighted and telling him it's an alligator.

**T** Taking down obscene poster from son's bulletin board just before party and substituting brochure for math camp.

**U** Unlocking bathroom door with an ice pick when a child just told you he's not doing anything only to discover he's not doing anything.

**V** Visiting child's unstable teacher at school and telling her, "I don't understand. He never acts like that at home."

**W** Writing a postdated check to the tooth fairy for a buck and a half.

**X** X-raying for a swallowed nickel only after you heard it was a collector's coin worth $6.40.

**Y** Yawning during school play when your daughter has the lead—a dangling participle.

**Z** Zipping last year's boots on your son when you know they will never come off without surgery.

**37**

*What kind of a mother would...*
**give up sighing for Lent... when she's Jewish?**

# Rose

Rose had been playing the game of "musical mother" for over five years now. Next to the lottery, it was the biggest game of the twentieth century. It required anywhere from two to eight players. The rules were simple.

Take one widowed mother and spin her around until she comes to rest with her daughter in Florida. Daughter in Florida has four months to con her brother in Chicago to take her. Brother in Chicago keeps her until he can spread fifty pounds of guilt on his sister in California.

The mother always loses. Rose had logged more air miles than a space shuttle astronaut.

Ever since the death of her husband Seymour, four years ago, Rose changed bedrooms every four months. She fantasized about a rest home and allowed herself the luxury of contemplating a room of her own—a place where she could talk when she felt like it and be surrounded by other people with irregularity problems.

Her children wouldn't hear of it. They had a responsibility to take care of her and she had the responsibility of enduring it.

Every night, no matter where she was, Rose indulged in the practice of calling on Seymour's presence for a nightly conversation.

## FLORIDA (July)

"So, it's Florida. It must be July. How are things with you, Seymour? Irene, Sam, and Sandy met me at the airport. Your grandson is a scarecrow. Twelve years old and he can't weigh more than fifteen pounds. How could he when there's nothing in this house to eat? All the bread is frozen and every box in the cupboard has grains of wheat growing on it and NATURAL stamped all over it. I don't want to worry you, but he'll be dead by Chanukah.

"I'm in the guest room, as usual. Remember the recovery room just before you died? Same decorator. They store everything here. I sleep next to a ping-pong table and an ironing board that hasn't been down since they moved here.

"Nothing has changed with Irene. Her ice cubes still smell like melon, and she thinks dust was put here to measure time. Where did we fail, Seymour? It's a good thing you aren't here to see it. The woman doesn't even wash her dishes in sudsy water and rinse them before putting them into the dishwasher.

"I have to go now. Irene is having theme week in the kitchen and tonight it's Korea's turn. I starve to death with chopsticks. See you later when the rates go down. That's a joke, Seymour."

## FLORIDA (October)

"You there, Seymour? So, how do you like my hair? Irene thought I ought to wear it pulled straight back and into a bun. I think it makes me look older. If you think it makes me look older, give me a sign, like lowering the humidity here to 96.

"I fainted twice today. Do you remember those copper-bottomed pots and pans we gave Irene for a wedding present? You wouldn't believe, Seymour. I saw them today and said, 'Tell me those aren't the pots and pans your father and I bought you.' She said, 'What's the matter with them?'

"I said, 'Would it kill you to sprinkle a little cleanser on them each time you use them? You weren't raised to let your bottoms go.'

"Nothing much happening. I paid my health insurance. Irene and Sam wanted me to go with them to the Levines' for dinner, but the last time we went out I was washing out cups in the sink and they were in the car blowing their horn at me and I almost passed out. It isn't worth the aggravation.

"I heard Sam on the phone talking with Russell, so it looks like I'll make my annual visit to Chicago. A lot of people winter there. Stay well."

## CHICAGO (November)

"Hello, Seymour. Guess who? There's something I've got to know. When you went to heaven, did you have a five-hour layover in Atlanta? If you did, I'm not coming.

"Your son looks good. Barbara looks as good as

can be expected. The children still have no necks. I wonder why that is. Russell has a neck. My theory is that all four of them are cold all the time and trying to keep warm.

"Barbara and I play thermostat roulette each night. I don't see how she stands it. She said the other night, 'It's healthy to sleep in a cool room.' I said, 'Who sleeps? I'm afraid to nod off or I'll never wake up again.' You remember that movie where it happened to Ronald Colman, don't you?

"So, the woman tries. Four children. She has her hands full trying to get David toilet trained. She got him a little potty seat that plays music when he tinkles. It should play 'The Impossible Dream.'

"And she waits on me hand and foot. Fills up my plate, does my laundry, reminds me to take my pills and turns my bed back into a sofa every time I go to the bathroom.

"Playing any golf? Talk to you soon."

# CHICAGO (February)

"Be honest with me, Seymour. Is it me? Or are the winters getting longer? I stood at the window today and for the life of me couldn't remember what green grass looked like. I asked Barbara and she just stood and looked at me. She probably can't remember, either. I paid my health insurance. Mostly, I watch a lot of soap operas. It's a shame you can't see them. They're enough to start your heart beating again. Went to the dentist today and he said I should have my bridgework redone. Hang onto your billfold, Seymour. It will cost $4,000.

"When I told Barbara she said, 'You're seventy-two years old. What do you want to get your teeth fixed for?'

"Russell talked with Judith today. He said she's lonely after the divorce and wants me to visit.

"All of a sudden, I feel very old and very tired. Maybe when I get to California, the smog, brush fires, floods, and earthquakes will cheer me up."

## CALIFORNIA (March)

"I know I just got here Seymour, but I had to talk with you. Our Judith has had a face lift. At forty-three, how far could it have fallen? I thought she looked different when I saw her. She has a surprised look on her face twenty-four hours a day.

"Your grandson Marty and I had a long talk coming in from the airport. I told him about my bridgework and he said the same thing you did—'Go for it.'"

## CALIFORNIA (April)

"Seymour, we've got to stop meeting like this. That's a joke. It's good to hear you laugh. I made a friend today. You know how I hate dryers, so I took a couple of Marty's shirts and stretched a line out back. I met a woman visiting her son next door and—are you ready? She hangs shirts by the tails, too, instead of the collar.

"She invited me to a funeral tomorrow. I might go . . . just to see something sagging again. You'll probably find out anyway, and I want you to hear it from me. Judith is dating a man called Patrick. I said to him, 'What's your family name?' He said, 'Murphy.' I said, 'What was it before?' He said, 'Before what?' I don't think he's Jewish. Why am I being punished?"

In May, Rose was suspicious that her life was about to change. Usually her trip to Florida was confirmed by this time.

There had been phone calls. A lot of them. Judith talked with Irene and Sam in low, serious voices at night. Russell and Barbara talked with Judith, who nodded occasionally and said, "I noticed."

In June, Judith summoned her mother to the kitchen for a talk. The entire family had noticed behavior that was "erratic." Barbara expressed concern that Rose stood near a window in Chicago and mumbled, "Admit it, God, Chicago was a big mistake!"

Irene had reported tearfully that she peeked in her room one night to find her in deep conversation with the ping-pong table. It was their consensus that Rose should be put in a home.

The room was sparse, but Rose could fix that. She'd get her rocker out of storage and some pillows and glassware she'd saved. But before she unpacked, she had to get in touch with Seymour. "You there?" she asked looking toward the ceiling.

"Listen, you're not going to believe this, but I had to go to Atlanta to get here. I'd have thought California to Colorado would have been a straight shot, wouldn't you?" Out of the corner of her eye, Rose noticed another resident of the home who had dropped by. "Wait a minute, Seymour, there's someone here."

Her visitor said, "You're talking to Seymour? My husband died two years ago and talks about a Seymour all the time. Does he play golf? What's his handicap?"

**38**

# "Do I Have to Use My Own Money?"

When the history of guilt is written, parents who refuse their children money will be right up there in the Top Ten.

When do you give it to them? And when do you stop? I read somewhere that you should set up an allowance system to instill in your children the basics of self-esteem.

I paid my kids to close their eyes, blow their noses, breathe in and out, clean out their cages, pick up their towels, keep their feet on the floor, and, one New Year's Day, when my head was very sensitive to sound, I offered one of them a blank check if he would stop smacking his lips.

By the time the kids hit puberty, they were filthy rich. The reason they were filthy rich is that they never spent their own money on anything.

Somehow I never got over the feeling of knowing he had $2,500 in his savings account and I got a paper doily basket with three black jelly beans for Mother's Day.

It was always "sticky" as to what they were financially responsible for.

Take the area code 602 with a 1 in front of it my son once dated. I mean, a 1-602 wasn't across a whole country from 602, but it was far enough away to run our phone bill up to $35 a month in long-distance charges.

It was a marriage made by Ma Bell between two people who shared such insights as:

"What are you doing?"

"Nothing. What are you doing?"

"I don't want to interrupt you if you're doing something."

"I told you I wasn't doing anything."

"You sure?"

"I'm sure."

"So, what are you doing?"

We never had to worry about the physical part of the relationship because they were never off the phone. He would set his alarm to call her in the morning. At night I would go into his room and remove the phone from his ear as he slept. It was like hanging up an umbilical cord. As soon as they left each other after school in the afternoon, he would shout, "I'll call you when I get home." I offered to feed him intravenously.

One day I approached him with the phone bill and suggested he pay for it with his own money. He smiled and said, "You think this is just some infatuation, don't you? You don't realize this is a person I genuinely care for and want to spend the rest of my life with. She's important to me and very special. There isn't anything I wouldn't do for her."

"I'm glad to hear you say that," I said, "because according to this bill you owe us $84.10 in long-distance telephone charges."

He never talked to her or saw her again.

All parents set their own goals as to when the Open Purse policy ends with their children.

Ours ended the day we knew in our hearts that our

son's savings account was the only thing between us and welfare benefits.

We made a speech: "We know you won't understand this now, but someday you will. We no longer want to deprive you of the poverty you so richly deserve. The Happy Days Are Here Again Bank of Prosperity is closed! Money is not related to love. It's only a shallow substitute. What you really need is a ton of self-respect."

He sat there for a while in silence. Finally he said, "Do I have to buy it with my own money?"

We smiled. "It's the only way you can buy it."

**39**

# The Spirit of Christmas...
# and Other Expenses

Every year, one of my children wants a game for Christmas. It is always one for which the demand exceeds the supply by about 355,000.

Every kid in town has it on his list.

The game is touted on television, beginning in June, with the approach that if it is not under your tree on Christmas Day you are an unfit parent and your child will grow up to rob convenience stores wearing pantyhose over his face.

By September, your child has built up to such a pitch that if he doesn't get this game, he may give up breathing. He assures you it is the only game he wants. Now the pressure is on you to find that game. For the purpose of avoiding a lawsuit, I will call the game Humiliation, fun for the entire family, order no. 170555354, batteries not included.

By October, every store in your area is sold out of Humiliation, with no hope of getting a new order in. But the television teasers go on, showing a typical American family with Mom, Dad, and 2.5 children sitting around a table playing Humiliation until they pass out from joy.

Forget baking fruitcake, buying a Christmas tree, entertaining with wassail, caroling, sending out Christmas cards, or decorating the house. Every morning as soon as the alarm goes off, your feet touch the floor and you give the battle cry, "Find Humiliation today!"

By mid-November, you have driven 1,800 miles in search of the game, following tips from friends that a discount house in the northern part of the state has two left, or a toy dealer has one under the counter that is damaged but negotiable.

Several times you are tempted to get a game that is a rip-off of Humiliation, like Mortify or Family Conceit, but you know in your heart it wouldn't be the same.

If you're lucky(?), just before Christmas you race a little old grandmother to the counter and snatch the last Humiliation game on Earth from her fingers, buy batteries and put it under the tree.

On Christmas night, while you're picking up all the paper, ribbon, and warranties, your eyes fall on Humiliation, still in the box, the $49.95 price tag shining like a beacon.

The kids are playing with a cardboard box and snapping the air pockets of plastic packing material. Humiliation had its minute and now it's gone.

Why do we do it?

How are we manipulated into buying toys we cannot afford and are interesting for a matter of minutes? Several reasons: For one, parents are basically insecure and have to buy affection, and second, we are cursed with short memories.

We refuse to stop and reflect on toys past that have been discarded.

Like the horse. Remember him? He was brown and sucked up eighty gallons of water a day through his face. He was a lot of fun and lived with us for three years. Every time the farrier came to shoe him, it cost $45. No one wanted to pick the manure out of his feet because it was "gross." He attracted flies and disliked the sensation of anything on his back. He was ridden twelve times.

Or the ping-pong table. It was a big table that held books, coats, dirty laundry, lunch bags, stuff that had to go to the cleaner, and stacks of old newspapers. You couldn't see the TV over it, and it eventually went to the garage, where it warped.

From Christmas past came a full set of leather-bound, gilt-edged encyclopedias containing 3,000 illustrations. These were supposed to bring a new level of culture to the family, and I recollect were used twice: first to point out pictures of Eve, who was naked in Volume V, and second, to hold open the door when the new sofa was delivered.

I recall the plastic inflatable swimming pool that was to bring the whole family closer together. It was officially dedicated on the morning of July 5 and officially closed on the evening of July 5, when it was noted that a small boy in the neighborhood had drunk five glasses of grape drink and had not left the pool in twelve hours.

The ice hockey sticks were biggies and are still in the closet awaiting the arrival of the Canadian Salvation Army. They fell from favor when it was discovered they did not have training wheels on them and worked only when someone stood upright on ice skates.

I try to be a good mother, a loving mother, a considerate mother, who wants to see her children happy.

That's too bad. Shallow and unfeeling is a lot cheaper.

**40**

*What kind of a mother would...*

**tell her children if they didn't come home for Christmas, she'd be dead by New Year's?**

# Mary

The four of them had been poring over the luncheon menu for fifteen minutes in total silence.

It was a waiting game to see who would ask the question first. Iris broke the ice. "Is anyone going to have the popovers?"

The question was ludicrous. Does Zsa Zsa Gabor refuse a proposal of marriage? No one in their right mind would come to Neiman Marcus's tea room in Atlanta and not order popovers.

"I don't know," mused Mary. "I'm cutting back, but maybe I'll have one just to be sociable."

The waitress shifted to the other foot. "You want your usual two baskets?" Everyone nodded.

How long had they been coming here? Twice a year for the last twelve or fifteen years? They gathered every June 3 on Jefferson Davis's birthday and January 10 to commemorate the birth of Robert E. Lee.

A lot had happened in those fifteen years. Their roots

had gone from black to gray and back to black again. Their children had gone from home to husbands and come home again. Their husbands from office to retirement to home, and their cars from station wagons with bad clutches to coupes with bad clutches.

"Another round of sherry from the bar?" asked the waitress.

"Why not?" said Charlotte. "After all, this is a festive occasion."

"Has anyone heard about Evelyn Rawleigh?" asked Iris.

"What happened?" asked Bebe.

"Well, she went through a series of the most awful allergy tests ever, only to discover she's allergic to ultra-suede."

They gasped as a quartet.

"I'd get a second opinion," said Bebe.

"How tragic," said Charlotte. "Is there nothing they can do for her?"

"Nothing," sighed Iris. "And the worst of it is she won't leave the house. She thinks everyone is looking at her."

The waitress returned with the sherry and Bebe made the toast, "To Robert E. Lee, who won the war. So, did everyone have a good Christmas?"

"I know Iris did," said Charlotte. "As usual, your Christmas Newsletter was inspired!"

God, how they all hated those Newsletters. Iris should have made *The New York Times* best-seller list for fiction. Who else had kids who were toilet trained at seven months, guest conductor for the Atlanta Symphony at six, and sent thank-you notes in French? Their family picture on the letter made the Osmond family look depressed. Was it their imagination, or did their teeth get straighter every year?

"Well, I had the best Christmas ever," volunteered Bebe. "Dede had us all over at her house. What a dear she is! I couldn't love her more if she were my own daughter. What about you, Mary? Any of your children come home?"

Home! Jeff had sent her a plastic salad spinner that you put your lettuce into to twirl all the water out. He called on Christmas Eve from Vail, where he'd gone with his family to unwind. How tightly wound could a thirty-four-year-old salesman of after-shave lotion get?

Jennifer had sent her an expensive executive organizer handbag with eighty-three compartments for the woman on the go. The only problem was she wasn't going anywhere.

Robin had been the biggest disappointment. She had sent salt and pepper shakers shaped like unicorns and a note that said, "These remind me of you and Dad. I love you. Robin."

The group was waiting for her answer. "You know how busy they are, but as usual they were too extravagant. Imagine designer chocolates when I told them I was counting calories."

Bebe summoned the waitress and ordered another round of sherry. Then, turning to Charlotte, she asked, "So how does Walter like retirement?"

Charlotte forced herself to smile. She had married Walter for better or for worse, but not for lunch. From the day he retired he had taken over her kitchen like a carpetbagger. The first week he was home she entered her kitchen and asked, "What do you think you are doing?"

He said, "If God permits me to live long enough, I am going to clean your exhaust fan. If I had run my office like you run your kitchen, Charlotte, we'd have starved to death years ago."

So Walter had alphabetized her spices and she drank

to "festive" occasions, which in recent months had included National Foot Health Week, the dedication of a sewage plant, and the day she got her fur out of storage.

"I never knew retirement could be so wonderful," she said and whispered to the waitress, "Bring the bottle."

"Is everyone as bored with TV as I am?" asked Iris. "I mean, you can't turn on a show anymore without all those disgusting people kissing with their mouths open."

"They're all doing it," said Bebe. "Even Carol Burnett."

"By the way, Iris," said Mary, "how's your daughter?"

Iris winced. At thirty-two, Constance had racked up two marriages, two meaningful relationships, one child, and a state of bankruptcy. On the Christmas Newsletter, this was translated as "Connie is in St. Louis working on a novel."

Charlotte nearly knocked over a glass of wine, catching it just in time. She put her finger to her lips, signaling secrecy. "Don't tell Walter. Did I tell you the other day he met me at the door and shouted, 'You have exactly three hours to do something with this yeast before the date on it expires'? I told him to take that yeast and . . ."

"Popovers, anyone?" asked Iris.

"You think you got problems," said Bebe. "That Yankee daughter-in-law of mine doesn't even trust me to diaper the baby. She said things have changed. The plumbing looked the same to me."

Mary spoke slowly and deliberately. "Do you ever get the feeling that none of this happened? That we put in thirty years of our lives and have nothing to show for it?"

"I love my children," said Iris defensively. "Even the ones who are shacking up."

"Mine never really knew me," Mary mumbled, as if talking to herself. "I never let them. I couldn't. I had to set the example. I had to make sure they saw only the best. I never cried in front of them. I never laughed when I wasn't supposed to. In all those years they never saw me without hair spray. What do you think of that?"

"That's wonderful," said Iris.

"That's lousy," said Mary. "Do you know what a unicorn is? It's a mys . . . mystical . . . weird animal with a horse's body and a horn on top that everyone needlepoints. Sort of aloof and unreal. There's nothing there to love. That's how Robin sees me. A unicorn. I was never real."

"What are we supposed to do with the rest of our lives?" mused Charlotte. "One minute there weren't enough hours in the day to do all I had to do. And the next thing I know I'm dressing all the naked dolls that belonged to my daughter and arranging them on the bed. Did you ever iron a bra for a two-inch bust? We're too young to pack it in and too old to compete for our own turf."

"Would we have done things differently if we had known then what we know now?" asked Charlotte.

For a full minute no one spoke.

"I'd have talked less and listened more," said Bebe.

"I'd have eaten more ice cream and less cottage cheese," said Charlotte.

"I'd never have bought anything that had to be ironed or was on sale," said Iris. "How about you, Mary?"

"I'd have been more human . . . and less unicorn."

Mary filled her wine glass and made a toast. "To the sainted mother of Robert E. Lee, who on this day gave birth to a legend. What do you want to bet that for Christmas she got a plastic salad spinner?"

**41**

*What kind of a mother would...*
**sentence her eighty-two-year-old**
**mother to Chez Riche, a $2,000-a-month**
**nursing home?**

# Ethel

Ethel refused to believe her mother was approaching senility.

She rationalized a lot of eighty-two-year-old women ran away from home every week, sat in parked cars talking to themselves, and threatened to name Cary Grant in a paternity suit.

She would not listen to anyone who advised her against keeping her mother at home with her. Not her doctor, her minister, her husband, nor her Aunt Helen who insisted, "Face it, Ethel, Jenny has one oar out of the water. She's my sister and I love her too, but I'm telling you normal people don't give out cans of tomato paste for Trick or Treat."

Ethel was defensive. "It's my fault. The kitchen was dark and she grabbed the first can she saw."

The burden of her mother's future was awesome to Ethel. When did the responsibility revert to her? Was it at her father's funeral three years ago when she put her arm around her mother and promised to take care of her? No, no, it was long before that that the mother became the child and the child became the mother.

She had started hearing echoes from her childhood soon after she was married.

"Mother! Aren't you ready yet? The doctor won't wait, you know." (Ethel! Don't dawdle. School will be over by the time you get there.)

"Come over Wednesday and I'll give you a permanent." (Hold still, Ethel, and I'll pin up your hair so you'll have curls.)

"Try this dress on, Mother. It'll make you look younger." (I don't care what you say, Missy, that dress is too old for you. Try this one.)

"Mother will have the fruit plate. She thinks she wants the veal parmesan but she'll be up all night." (I know a little girl whose eyes are bigger than her tummy.)

Her mother resisted at first, then fell easily into the role. After a while, when the memory went, Ethel was dialing phone numbers for her mother, filling her coffee cup half full, and automatically holding out her arm whenever she brought the car to a stop.

The transfer of authority was complete.

The lapses of her mother's memory were erratic. One minute Jenny could recall bite for bite what she had to eat forty years ago at a dinner at the VFW. The next minute, she was referring to her grandson as "Whatshisname." Ethel couldn't count the number of times her mother had thrown out the inside of the percolator with the grounds.

In time, she turned quarrelsome, irritable, and downright hostile toward Ethel. She announced to anyone who would listen that Ethel was stealing her blind and was trying to do her in by putting something bitter in her bran. She told her sister Helen, "I'd rather die of irregularity than be poisoned."

One night before guests, she tearfully told them she had been tortured beyond belief by her daughter, who had made her watch an Ali MacGraw film festival on TV.

The accusations broke Ethel's heart. Things came to a head one day, when her husband brought Jenny home from the polls where she had just voted. "Something has got to be done about Jenny," he said.

"What's the matter?" asked Ethel.

"She just voted Democrat. She'd die if she knew that."

Eight months later, Ethel checked her mother in at the Tranquil Trail Nursing Home. As they carried in her suitcase, Ethel observed, "It's a nice room, Mother."

"It's bugged," she said, "and it's dinky. Why didn't you just put me on an iceberg and let me drift out to sea. That's what Eskimos do."

"I wouldn't do that, Mother," she said tiredly.

"I suppose you've sold all my cut glass. You'll be old someday."

"I'm old now, Mother."

"That's true. Did you pack my fur coat?"

"It's July. You don't need it now. I'll bring it to you when it gets cold."

"You've said *that* before. Why don't you admit it. You sold it."

Ethel leaned back in the chair and rested her head. Was there anything left in her but frustration, hurt, and shame?

She was doing a terrible thing. She was abandoning her own mother, putting her in the hands of strangers. Her mother had sacrificed her entire life to raising her and now Ethel was turning away from her responsibilities. But she was so exhausted trying to relate to a person she didn't even know.

Her mother was living in a strange new world and had been for some time. It was a world that allowed the past to enter but not the present or the future. She had tried, but she couldn't reach her there. Nor did she want to. She wanted the old world. The way it used to be when her mother was softer and in control.

Would these strangers understand her mother's world?

An attendant came in and said, "Jenny, you got everything you need?"

"Did you steal my watch?" asked Jenny, her eyes narrowing.

"You bet. Was it valuable?"

Jenny stood toe to toe with her and searched her eyes carefully. "I got it from Cary Grant. I named him in a paternity suit and he tried to buy me off."

"Same thing happened to me with Clint Eastwood," said the attendant.

Together they walked out the door as Jenny whispered, "Clint Eastwood. Is he the one who squints all the time?"

Ethel watched them for a while, then wiped the tears from her eyes and put herself together. Maybe it would work. Maybe she was a constant reminder to her mother of the old world, the one that had left her suspicious and confused. Maybe that's why she lashed out at her with such anger. Oh well, she would think about it tomorrow, when she brought her mother's fur coat to her.

**42**

*What kind of a mother would . . .*

**reply when asked what it was like to give birth to Erma Bombeck, "It's a rotten job, but someone had to do it"?**

# Erma

This book would not be complete without a chapter on my mother, who at this moment is leafing through it to see if she is mentioned.

Words that flash through my mind when the word "Mother" is mentioned include: box saver, gravy on diet bread, right words in wrong places ("Your grandfather migrained here from Ireland"), candidate for first tongue transplant, courage, abounding love.

My mother was raised in an orphanage, married at fourteen, and widowed at twenty-five, left with two children and a fourth-grade education. According to her height and weight as listed on the insurance charts, she should be a guard for the Lakers. She has iron-starved blood, one shoulder that is lower than the other, and she bites her fingernails.

She is the most beautiful woman I have ever seen.

I never can remember exactly how old she is, so I set it at thirty-three and forget it.

In the years I was growing up, there were good times and bad times, but when I presented her with three children, our relationship stabilized. There is no doubt that the grandchildren offered her the answer to her prayers: revenge.

No one is more supportive of the First Amendment guaranteeing freedom of speech than I am, but the "gag rule" seems to get more attractive all the time.

When my kids are around, Grandma sings like a canary.

I never thought she'd turn on me. When I was sinking in a sea of diapers, formulas, and congenital spitting, Mother couldn't wait to pull her grandchildren onto her lap and say, "Let me tell you how rotten your Mommy was. She never took naps and she never picked up her room and she had a mouth like a drunken sailor in Shanghai. I washed her mouth out with soap so many times I finally had to starch her tongue."

At other times, she is on my side and her presence is comforting.

Once, when I was in my twenties, I remember standing in a hospital corridor waiting for doctors to put twenty-one stitches in my son's head and I said, "Mom, when do you stop worrying?" She just smiled and said nothing.

When I was in my thirties, I sat on a little chair in a classroom and heard how one of my children talked incessantly, disrupted the entire class, and was headed for a career making license plates. I said to her, "Mom, when does it end?" She said nothing.

When I was in my forties, I spent a lifetime waiting for the phone to ring, the cars to come home, the front door to open. I called her and whined, "When does it stop?" There was no answer.

By the time I was fifty, I was sick and tired of being

vulnerable and worrying about my children. I wished they were all married so I could stop worrying and lead my own life. But I was haunted by my mother's smile and I couldn't help remembering how she looked at me with concern and said, "You look pale; you all right? Call me the moment you get home. I worry about it."

She had been trying to tell me what I did not want to hear: "It never stops."

When my first book came out, she went with me to New York, where my baptism on television was to be "The Tonight Show." I was terrified. As she was zipping me into my dress, I said, "I don't think I can do this," and she turned me around and said, "If you're going out there and try to be something you're not, you're right. You'll fall flat on your face. All you can do is to be yourself."

I went out that night and took her advice. I was myself. And I bombed so bad it was ten years before I ever got on the show again.

When I confronted Mother, she said, "What do I know? I just came along to shop at Bloomingdale's."

There's a lot to admire in my mother. The wonder she sustains . . . even at the age of thirty-three. She is still impressed with people, curious about new things, and excited about Christmas. Her openness is not to be believed. One day, a reporter from a supermarket tabloid knocked at her door and wanted to know anything about her daughter that the public didn't know. Mother invited him in, gave him coffee, told him my life story—beginning with the labor pains—in great detail. By the end of three hours (she was up to toilet training), his teeth were falling asleep and as he begged to leave, Mother insisted he take a bag of homemade raisins. He never came back.

I suppose every child remembers some special virtue their mother has—some piece of wisdom that has saved them from disaster or a word that made the path infinitely easier.

I love my mother for all the times she said absolutely nothing.

The times when I fell flat on my face, made a lousy judgment, and took a stand that I had to pay dearly for.

God knows I've made every mistake in the book, from the time I bought a car with 87,000 miles on it to the time I made a decision to tell my boss, "I don't need this job."

Thinking back on it all, it must have been the most difficult part of mothering she ever had to do: knowing the outcome, yet feeling she had no right to keep me from charting my own path.

I thank her for all her virtues, but mostly for never once having said, "I told you so."

# Epilogue

While the Good Lord was creating mothers He was into His sixth day of "overtime" when the angel appeared and said, "You're doing a lot of fiddling around on this one."

And the Lord said, "Have you read the spec on this order?"

She has to be completely washable, but not plastic.

Have 180 movable parts . . . all replaceable.

Run on black coffee and leftovers.

Have a lap that disappears when she stands up.

Have a kiss that can cure anything from a broken leg to a disappointed love affair.

And have six pairs of hands.

The angel shook her head slowly and said, "Six pairs of hands . . . not possible."

"It's not the hands that are causing me problems," said the Lord. "It's the three pairs of eyes that mothers have to have."

"That's on the standard model?" asked the angel.

The Lord nodded. "One pair that see through closed doors when she asks, 'What are you kids doing in there?' when she already knows. Another here in the back of her head that see what she shouldn't, but what she has to know, and of course the ones here in front that can look at a child when he goofs up and reflect, 'I understand and I love you' without so much as uttering a word."

"Lord," said the angel, touching His sleeve gently, "come to bed. Tomorrow . . ."

"I can't," said the Lord, "I'm so close to creating something so close to myself. Already I have one who heals herself when she is sick . . . can feed a family of six on one pound of hamburger . . . and can get a nine-year-old to stand under a shower."

The angel circled the model of The Mother very slowly. "It's too soft," she sighed.

"But tough," said the Lord excitedly. "You cannot imagine what this Mother can do or endure."

"Can it think?"

"Not only think, but it can reason and compromise," said the Creator.

Finally, the angel bent over and ran her fingers across the cheek. "There's a leak," she pronounced. "I told you you were trying to put too much into this model. You can't ignore the stress factor."

The Lord moved in for a closer look and gently lifted the drop of moisture to his finger where it glistened and sparkled in the light.

"It's not a leak," He said. "It's a tear."

"A tear?" asked the angel. "What's it for?"

"It's for joy, sadness, disappointment, compassion, pain, loneliness, and pride."

"You are a genius," said the angel.

The Lord looked somber. "I didn't put it there."

## About the Author

ERMA BOMBECK writes a humor column three times a week for 900 newspapers from her home in Paradise Valley, Arizona. She appears twice a week on ABC's *Good Morning America*. She has a loving husband and three children who have never published a book about her. She calls her Mom and Dad at least once a week and holds ten honorary degrees.

Her husband comes home everyday and asks, "So, what have you been doing all day?"